Create Your Own

Home Networks

ELI LAZICH

SAMS   800 East 96th Street, Indianapolis, Indiana 46240

Create Your Own Home Networks

International Standard Book Number: 0-672-32832-1

Library of Congress Catalog Card Number: 2005934065

Printed in the United States of America

First Printing: November 2005

08   07   06   05   4   3   2   1

Trademarks

All terms mentioned in this book that are known to be trademarks or service marks have been appropriately capitalized. Sams Publishing cannot attest to the accuracy of this information. Use of a term in this book should not be regarded as affecting the validity of any trademark or service mark.

Warning and Disclaimer

Every effort has been made to make this book as complete and as accurate as possible, but no warranty or fitness is implied. The information provided is on an "as is" basis. The author(s) and the publisher shall have neither liability nor responsibility to any person or entity with respect to any loss or damages arising from the information contained in this book.

Bulk Sales

Sams Publishing offers excellent discounts on this book when ordered in quantity for bulk purchases or special sales. For more information, please contact

U.S. Corporate and Government Sales
1-800-382-3419
corpsales@pearsontechgroup.com

For sales outside of the U.S., please contact

International Sales
international@pearsoned.com

Publisher
Paul Boger

Acquisitions Editor
Neil Rowe

Development Editor
Mark Renfrow

Managing Editor
Charlotte Clapp

Project Editor
George Nedeff

Copy Editor
Kitty Jarrett

Indexer
Chris Barrick

Proofreader
Elizabeth Scott

Technical Editor
J. Boyd Nolan

Publishing Coordinator
Cindy Teeters

Book Designer
Gary Adair

Contents at a Glance

Table of Contents

About the Author

Eli Lazich has been either supporting or teaching computer networking for more than 20 years. His interest in computer networking started even before he had his first real job but came to fruition when he was part of a team that implemented a Novell NetWare ELS system. Eli is a Certified Novell Engineer and Instructor (CNE and CNI) and a Microsoft Certified System Engineer and Trainer (MCSE and MCT). He is proficient with all the Microsoft Windows operating systems, including Windows XP. Other operating systems with which he has worked and written software include Linux, FreeBSD, and BSD/OS. Eli currently runs a home network of his own, implementing projects found in this book as well as some other fun things.

Dedication

I dedicate this book to my muse, best friend, and the embodiment of my ideal in a woman, my wife Kathy. You have been an ardent supporter and champion of mine in all situations. You have taught me more than I ever imagined and still can surprise me after 13 years of marriage. Thank you for all the memories created in the past and those that are yet to come. I tell you this all the time, but I don't think I will ever be able to completely express to you how much I love you.

Acknowledgments

I'd like to thank my children, Hannah, Jonah, Sophia, and Tessa. They have each in their own unique way not only enriched my life by their mere presence but also nurtured my mind, body, and spirit. I am thrilled by the people they already are and am excited at the prospect of who they will become. I am proud of each of them for the fiercely independent spirit that they demonstrate.

I'd like to also thank my agent, Neil Salkind, at StudioB, for all his tireless work in seeking out writing opportunities. This was a fun book to be involved with, and I look forward to many more projects under his guidance.

Finally, I would like to thank the folks at Sams Publishing for putting this book together. Neil Rowe and Mark Renfrow are the two people with whom I worked directly, and I thank them both for their communication, feedback, and getting this project completed.

We Want to Hear from You!

As the reader of this book, *you* are our most important critic and commentator. We value your opinion and want to know what we're doing right, what we could do better, what areas you'd like to see us publish in, and any other words of wisdom you're willing to pass our way.

As an associate publisher for Sams Publishing, I welcome your comments. You can email or write me directly to let me know what you did or didn't like about this book—as well as what we can do to make our books better.

Please note that I cannot help you with technical problems related to the topic of this book. We do have a User Services group, however, where I will forward specific technical questions related to the book.

When you write, please be sure to include this book's title and author as well as your name, email address, and phone number. I will carefully review your comments and share them with the author and editors who worked on the book.

Email: feedback@samspublishing.com

Mail: Paul Boger
          Publisher
          Sams Publishing
          800 East 96th Street
          Indianapolis, IN 46240 USA

For more information about this book or another Sams Publishing title, visit our website at www.samspublishing.com. Type the ISBN (excluding hyphens) or the title of a book in the Search field to find the page you're looking for.

INTRODUCTION

INTRODUCTION

This book provides you with a guide to some of the most productive, interesting, and just plain fun things you can do with your computers. Many people these days have more than one computer at home and can easily become bewildered by all the possibilities. The topics covered in this book will take you from the basics of computer networking to how to use your computer to accomplish many everyday home networking tasks.

Along the way, this book provides you with enough extra information in the form of side-bars to either pique your interest or satisfy your curiosity, depending on your level of interest in the topic. Because I am firmly convinced that people learn best by actually performing a task rather than simply reading about it, this book provides detailed, step-by-step procedures that show you exactly what to click or type to achieve the desired result. It also provides web links along the way, where appropriate. When you have your home network set up, you can follow these links to get more information.

The most important assumption this book makes is that you are using Windows XP as your operating system and that you are famil-iar with the basic operation and functionality it offers. This book does not cover any back-ground operating system concepts, but many fine books are available to help you with that sort of information (for example, *Sams Teach Yourself Windows XP All in One* from Sams Publishing). Most of the projects presented in this book can be accomplished by using what ships (and should be installed) with your copy of Windows XP. Where appropriate, this book tells you where and how to obtain any other software and then describes how to install it.

The five projects described in this book are designed to build on a common foundation. You will first implement a network for your home computers to enable connectivity. You will learn enough background information to understand the underlying rationale for what you are doing. To build on the network founda-tion, you will then enable sharing of informa-tion and devices. In the next project, you will learn how to share music on your network, as well as how to import music from various loca-tions to the computers on your network. This is followed by a project where you will enable instant real-time communications with users on your network as well as the Internet at large. You will then see how to make your home videos available across your network. You'll find guidance on problems that commonly occur in networks and how to resolve them. Finally, the last chapter shows you how to use your computers to create your own website.

You can do many more things with the solu-tions described in this book. So as you read through these chapters and work through the projects, you should think beyond the projects and look for more, related information, either on your own or with the help of a well-placed Internet search engine query. Finally, because I am a fan of philosophy, I ask that you keep in mind that the journey is the destination.

CHAPTER 1

Understanding Basic Networking

You have accumulated two or more computers, and you've decided to connect them together, so welcome to the wonderful world of creating your own home network! You are in for some fun, productive use of your time, as well as the occasional aggravations that comes with such an endeavor. Then again, nothing worth doing is always easy, is it?

Computers enable us to accomplish many useful tasks, and as standalone devices, they are quite extraordinary. However, when computers can communicate and share or exchange information, some of the things we take for granted, and indeed some of the most amazing tasks, can be accomplished. These days we send mail electronically, and it is received in seconds rather than days. As a matter of fact, nowadays we can communicate in real time with instant messaging rather than even having to wait for email to reach the recipient. In some cases, entire books are created without the creators being in the same room. As a matter of fact, many books are written without the authors or any of the people involved in the publishing process ever meeting face-to-face. Family reunions, birthday parties, camping trips, kids' sporting events, and many other activities can be easily shared with distant relatives by means of the Internet. The limits are literally as varied as your imagination. So while this book will show you how to accomplish a few of the tasks possible with a network, it is by no means exhaustive. I encourage you to use the wealth of knowledge available on the Internet to satisfy your curiosity. Start with an idea or a question and then use one of the search engines, such as Google, to take off from there.

In this chapter, we need to establish an understanding of what *networking* is, in the context of computers. We'll cover a little bit of the conceptual by exploring networking with the perceptual; that is, you'll learn by doing. To get started, let's cover some of the concepts and terminology that is typically used in the world of computer networking.

Getting Computers to Communicate

Over the years, we humans have developed language as a means of communication to enable understanding of the things we perceive around us. We have developed perceptions into concepts, which we convey to our fellow humans by using language. We have developed a high-level language to convey complex conceptual abstractions.

In the development of any language, a commonality must exist so that the various parties involved in the conversation are able to understand each other. We can think of this as the *protocol* of the spoken language. For example, the English language follows a structure: We need to include nouns, verbs, and adjectives in the expected locations in our sentences (both spoken and written) so that our intended audience can follow what we are talking about. Imagine someone speaking and using nothing but verbs, such as "walk swam running fell punched." This is an arbitrary collection of words, and without the proper context, you would have no idea what the speaker was talking about. Figure 1.1 shows what can be considered an orderly conversation between humans. The people in the conversation follow a typical process of speaking and/or listening. After a period of processing, responses come from the other party, and the conversation continues.

FIGURE 1.1

Human communication.

How was your weekend?

Fine, thanks. How was yours?

Good, we went to our cabin and did a bit of fishing with the kids. What were you up to?

We installed a new water garden and did a bit of landscaping.

As in human language, communication in computer networking requires some fundamentals. It needs a medium of some sort on which communications can take place. When people communicate, the air around us can be considered the communications medium. (So in a sense, we have been using wireless networking for quite some time.) Using our sense of hearing, we are able to tune in—and sometimes tune out—what others are saying. In a computer network, we use something known as *Ethernet*, which involves just a wire that looks very much like a telephone wire connected to computers by means of a network interface card (NIC). You can think of a NIC as the computer equivalent of ears. Recently, wireless networking has gained a great deal of popularity. Even in a wireless network, a computer must have a NIC in order to communicate with other computers. Radio frequencies are used in the case of wireless networking to establish communications between computers. Figure 1.2 shows a typical computer network. Computers follow a very orderly process when they communicate. For example, if Computer A were sending data, all the other computers would listen and process that data. Just as humans wait for cues in a conversation to let them know that someone has finished speaking, computers act on the electronic equivalent of such cues to determine when another computer has finished communicating.

> **NOTE**
>
> Computer communications are actually quite a bit more orderly than human communications. In human conversations, people often interrupt the speaker. In computer communications, the rules of data transmission define how each computer should participate in communication and recover if something goes wrong. So we usually don't encounter an interruption in computer communications and when we do, they don't lose their place in the conversation. If only our own conversations were so efficient.

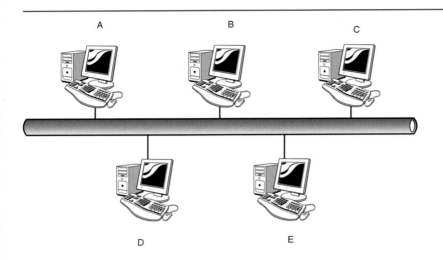

FIGURE 1.2

A typical computer network.

In computer networking, we also need a language of sorts in order to use computers to share and exchange information. This language should follow a certain convention, or *protocol*, so that the computers involved in the electronic conversation are able to decode information received from other computers. What we are referring to here in fairly broad generalizations is covered by what is known as the Open Systems Interconnect (OSI) computer networking model. (You can do a quick search on Google or any other search engine for *OSI* to find more detailed information.)

One of the protocols that emerged from the OSI body of work is referred to as Transmission Control Protocol/Internet Protocol (TCP/IP). Today, TCP/IP is the prevalent computer networking protocol. As a matter of fact, the Internet is based on TCP/IP. TCP/IP is a communications protocol that encompasses how computers are addressed as well as how they exchange information in an orderly fashion. Each computer must identify the

computer with which it is exchanging information by means of an address. This is very much like dialing a friend's telephone number when you feel like discussing the day's activities. Instead of the well-known 7- or 10-digit telephone numbers, TCP/IP uses what an *IP address*. For example, 192.168.2.200 uniquely identifies a particular computer on a wired or wireless network. When making a telephone call, you sometimes need to dial an area code when calling someone outside your local calling zone. Similarly, TCP/IP identifies a portion of the address as the network portion. You will see this referred to as the *subnet mask*. For example, the address 192.168.2.200 contains information about both the network on which it is located and the individual computer to which it refers. The subnet mask for this address might be expressed as 255.255.255.0; to interpret this, wherever you see a 255, you assign that number to the network portion of the address, and wherever you see a 0, you assign that portion of the address to the individual computer. So our example address would be on the 192.168.2 network, which is shared by a number of computers. Each computer would maintain its own individual address on that network, and the computer in our example has the address 200.

Let's continue with the telephone analogy. Many telephones provide a feature whereby you can store a frequently dialed number and reference it by a name. The Internet uses the domain name system (DNS) so that you are not required to remember that 207.46.198.30 (at the time of this writing) is the IP address for one of Microsoft's web servers; all you have to remember is to type www.microsoft.com into the address field of your web browser, and you are connected to the site.

Why Set Up a Home Network?

Now that we've looked at some of the theory of computer networking, let's look at home networking from a practical perspective. The reasons for creating a home network can vary greatly. The following are some examples of what you can do with a home network:

▶ Share a single Internet connection among many computers

▶ Play computer games with friends and family members

▶ Enjoy your favorite audio and/or video content from any room in the house

▶ Print documents from any computer

▶ Collaborate with friends on homework

▶ Create your own personal website

TCP/IP ADDRESSES

In the early days of the Internet, when the only use for it was as a university research project, addresses were easy to get. There were only four universities on what would eventually become the worldwide Internet as we now know it. As the concept caught on, however, more and more schools, government institutions, and commercial enterprises saw the potential of the Internet and adopted its use in great numbers.

You have seen examples of IP address in this book; they generally take the form *w.x.y.z*, which is often referred to as *dotted-decimal notation*. This is basically the human-readable format for a binary number 32 bits in length. Recall that a binary number has only two states: It is either a 0 or a 1, which means it is either on or off.

There are 2^{32} (4,294,967,296) IP addresses available. While this seems like an inexhaustible supply, there are a few factors to be aware of. IP addresses in the current implementation (IP version 4) are broken up by classes:

▶ Class A addresses—In a Class A address, the first 8 bits (equivalent to the *w* in the *w.x.y.z* notation) refer to the network number.

▶ Class B addresses—Class B networks are identified by the fact that the first 16 bits (equivalent to the *w.x* in the *w.x.y.z* notation) refer to the network number.

▶ Class C addresses—Class C networks are identified by the fact that the first 24 bits (equivalent to the *w.x.y* in the *w.x.y.z* notation) refer to the network number.

continues

TCP/IP ADDRESSES *continued*

▶ **Class D and E addresses—Class D and E networks exist but are not used for general communication purposes.**

The Internet has grown and continues to grow at a tremendous rate, and we will in the not-too-distant future use up the supply of IP version 4 addresses.

To solve this impending problem, IP version 6 is in development. In IP version 6 there will be 128 bits used for an address, which means there can be 3.4×10^{38} unique addresses. This means that there are enough addresses in IP version 6 to accommodate each grain of sand on 300 million planets the size of Earth, assuming that the Earth were made entirely out of 1 cubic millimeter grains of sand. Suffice it to say, that is a lot of addresses, and we shouldn't run out any time soon. Personally, I'm looking forward to the possibility of having my own IP address brain implant and the ability to address all my devices with that implant.

If this sort of information really floats your boat (as it does mine), you owe it to yourself to get a copy of the late W. Richard Stevens's *TCP/IP Illustrated*, Volume 1, which covers every aspect of TCP/IP in minute detail. You can also do a search online to get more information about IP version 6.

▶ Share photographs with family members and friends

If you run a business out of your home, the advantages of a home network should be obvious: Everything that makes a business run—including communications, advertising, and financial transactions—is carried out on the Internet daily. Home networks are also handy for non-business use. If you have a single computer connected to the Internet, scheduling conflicts are bound to arise. Mom may be surfing the Internet, with Dad waiting his turn and the kids wanting to see the latest music video or play the latest game online at the same time. Even with multiple computers in the household, this situation can easily arise if there is but a single conduit to the Internet. Further, without a network, printer access is limited to the person whose computer the printer is connected to. All these potential aggravations can be solved by installing your own home network.

NOTE

As an example of one of the idiosyncrasies that technology brings to the table, my wife and I were both in the same house recently, using two different computers. Rather than calling out to me as we might have done in the past, my wife used instant messaging to send a text message to my screen. While this may seem trivial, the power that such a technology offers should not be overlooked. Without having to interrupt in any appreciable way what either of us were doing at the time, we were able to communicate very effectively.

Setting up a home network requires a bit of thought. You need to think about what your needs are, and then you need to decide what devices you need to purchase in order to connect your computers. The following are some of the items you might need:

► A wireless access point (WAP)
► A wireless network card(s)
► An Ethernet hub or switch
► A DSL or cable modem
► A NIC for wired solutions
► Category 5 Ethernet wires

This list is a starting point for the items to consider for your network. As your network matures and possibly becomes more sophisticated, you can add to this list as you see fit.

Security

The Internet is a rich medium. However, with the widespread access and anonymity offered by the Internet come security concerns. You want to be certain that when you perform a bank transaction, your privacy is maintained. You want to provide easy access to the wealth of information available on the Internet, but you don't want your kids exposed to objectionable material. You want to be reasonably assured that while you are exploring the wonder of the Internet, your computer is not subjected to malicious software such as viruses that could cause irreparable harm. These are but a few of the things you need to keep in mind as you think about securing your home computers.

A *firewall* is the basic device used to provide a measure of security on your network. *Virus scanners* and *spyware detectors* are also invaluable on the modern Internet. Many of the threats you encounter on the Internet can be dealt with by using a commonsense approach. The others require that you use the available technology. In no case, however, should you blindly trust technology to protect you without some knowledge of the harm that could come to your computers.

This book focuses on networking with the Microsoft Windows operating system. You'll want to keep abreast of security concerns and updates. You can do this through the Windows Update feature that is built in to Windows XP. Windows XP provides Windows Firewall, and you should certainly implement it for computers directly connected to the Internet. Windows XP also offers Internet Connection Sharing (ICS), which you should use if you use your Windows computer as the device directly connected to your ISP. ICS enables you to share a single Internet connection among all the computers in your network. You should regularly visit www.microsoft.com/security to stay informed of issues relating to security in general and in particular with the Windows operating systems.

Deciding How to Set Up Your Home Network

The items you need to set up a home network vary, depending on your goals. Assuming that you want your home network to be able to access the Internet, the first thing you need is an Internet connection to a local provider. The

Security is a huge issue any time you connect a computer to a network. There is an old saying that says the only way to completely secure a computer is to lock it away in a closet and not turn it on. Security requires a mindset in terms of computing. You need to weigh the pros and cons of security measures rather than blindly implementing solutions just because you may have heard that it is the ultimate security solution. There is no such thing as a panacea when it comes to computers, much as in life itself. The questions you should be asking yourself when you think about computer security should be much the same as those you consider when it comes to your home's security. For example, what am I trying to protect and from whom or what am I trying to protect it? Once you answer those questions, you are equipped to determine the tools available to address your concerns. There are some basic staple items when it comes to computer security, viruses and firewalls. Virus scanners are an essential tool as the prevalence of new malicious software is a continuing threat. Many vendors offer virus scanners, Norton and Computer Associates to name just a couple. Also keep in mind that security solutions such as virus scanners are a fluid process and must continually be updated. Be sure that you understand how to update your virus software. Also be sure that you understand how to update your Operating System. Microsoft's Windows Update website is a site you should be visiting regularly to ensure that you have the latest security updates for your computer. A firewall is another vital tool in your security arsenal. The basic approach of a firewall is to prevent any communication either to or from

continues

range of Internet connectivity is wide. Some of the most popular (high-speed) choices are digital subscriber line (DSL), cable broadband (typically from your cable provider), and satellite connections. In just about all cases, you need a *modem*. The modem connects your Ethernet port to your Internet service provider (ISP). In a single computer installation, you connect an Ethernet wire directly from your computer to this port.

What You Need for a Wired Network

If wired networking is your solution of choice, you need a few basic pieces of equipment. Many computers these days come equipped with Ethernet NICs preinstalled, so you may not need to purchase any when you decide to network your computers. Ethernet NICs need to be connected together using Ethernet cables, so you need the cables and a means of connecting your computers to each other. Therefore, you need to either locate all your computers in the same room or run wire behind walls so that all your computers can be connected to the network. The simplest method of connecting your computers over Ethernet is by using an Ethernet crossover cable to connect two computers. If you have more than two computers, you may need to purchase an Ethernet hub or switch. In this case, the computers in your home network would use an Ethernet cable to plug in to one of the open ports on the hub or switch.

Again, you need the following elements for a wired solution:

- ▸ A NIC for each computer
- ▸ Category 5 Ethernet wires
- ▸ An Ethernet hub or switch
- ▸ A router (whose function could be provided by your DSL or cable modem)

What You Need for a Wireless Network

If wireless networking is in your plans, you need a wireless NIC for each computer. These vary from a PC card for your laptop computers to PCI or USB wireless NICs for your desktop computers. In any case, you need a WAP, which is the wireless equivalent of an Ethernet hub or switch in that it connects computers that have wireless NICs. WAPs vary in their functionality, and you need to refer to the manufacturer's instructions for your specific device. In general, a WAP will be plugged in to the Ethernet port of the modem your ISP provides. (Chapter 2, "Project 1: Making Your Computers Talk to Each Other," covers more details about the various wireless solutions available.) The great advantage of wireless networking is that it enables you to put computers anywhere within range of your network. Figure 1.3 shows a typical layout of a home network. This network uses a wireless router as the means for the computers to access the Internet.

your computer unless explicitly allowed. With that knowledge in mind, once you do allow for some form of communication, either outbound or inbound, you are opening your computer to potential attacks. Keeping yourself informed is key to being able to keep your computer secure. Check a search engine such as Google for security, viruses, attacks, etc.

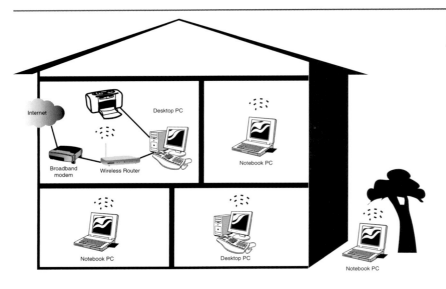

FIGURE 1.3

A typical home network.

It would be possible to substitute a computer for the wireless router shown in Figure 1.3. If you chose this option, your computer would become the router shown in this figure and would need two network cards installed. One NIC would connect to your modem and the other to your hub, switch, or WAP.

This book assumes that you'll create a network by using a wireless router that is directly connected to the ISP connection (as represented in Figure 1.3 by the broadband modem). The reason for choosing such an approach is the sheer simplicity with which connections can be made. With a wireless network, you do not need to be concerned with running any cables from your computers to a central switch or hub. And adding new computers to your network is as simple as adding a wireless network card to each new computer and turning it on.

Summary

Now that you have a basic understanding of computer networking, the rest of this book concentrates on how to get your computers communicating with each other. Then you can move on to the various fun and productive things you can do with your home network. Of course you will learn how to configure your computers to surf the Web; you will also learn how to share things like printers, photographs, and music among your home network computers. You will even take a brief look at how to create and share your own videos. Along the way, you'll have the opportunity to explore some things in more detail or go to Internet locations to read more about a particular topic.

Each of the following five chapters is a project. Each of the projects includes tasks that provide step-by-step instructions for achieving the desired results.

CHAPTER 2

Project 1: Making Your Computers Talk to Each Other

In Chapter 1, "Understanding Basic Networking," we touched on wired and wireless networks and some of the features of each. In this chapter we will begin to build a network solution that we will use as the basis for the rest of the projects in this book. Before we dive in, let's take a look at both wired and wireless solutions in a bit more detail. When you know more about what each solution offers, you will be better equipped to decide which is the best solution for your environment.

Understanding Network Speeds

When network optimization is discussed, you often hear terms relating to the speed of the network, in bits per second. For example, 10Mbps, which is the entry-level Ethernet network speed, refers to the network being capable of transferring information at the rate of 10 megabits per second, or 10 million bits per second. So what does this really mean to you?

Let's consider something that you might typically work with on a daily basis, such as a document written in Microsoft Word. A single-page Word document is about 20KB to 25KB in size. (A kilobyte roughly translates to 1,000 bytes.) We have a measurement mismatch here: We speak of network speeds in terms of megabits, but files are referred to in terms of kilobytes and sometimes megabytes. The basic difference here is that we are speaking of bits in one case and bytes in the other.

Bits and Bytes

Let's make sure we are clear about what each of these relatively obscure terms—*bits* and *bytes*—refers to:

▶ A *bit* is a single binary representation of information in electronic terms. A bit has one of two possible states: either a one (1) or a zero (0). The bit is either on (1) or off (0), sort of like a light switch.

▶ A *byte*, on the other hand, is a collection of 8 bits and can have one of 256 possible values.

Let's revisit that Word document again. That file, expressed in bits, is 20 bytes × 8 bits per byte = 160 bits. Simple math shows that this file takes but a fraction of a second to be transferred across a 10Mbps connection.

Let's look at another example. A digital photograph takes about 500 kilobytes of storage, depending on the resolution; the higher the quality of the picture, the more storage space required. This file represents 4000Kb, or 4Mb, of data. This file will take just under half of a second to transfer across a 10Mbps connection. This should give you a good idea of how to relate the terms you see thrown about when talking about network speeds. As long as all the computers on your network share the same connection speed, you have a reliable standard by which to judge connectivity.

Your connection to the Internet will typically be quite a bit slower than your local home network speed. DSL, cable, and satellite Internet connections run at speeds up to 1.5Mbps. For Web surfing, email, and file downloads, this speed is fine for most networks. As a matter of fact, you can stream audio and video with this type of Internet connection. You get the idea by now: Things really don't take that long to move across the network.

Next, let's turn our attention to the details of the various network types you'll typically use in a home environment.

Wired Ethernet Networking

Ethernet technologies are by far the most popular for home and small-business solutions. There are a number of Ethernet solutions from which you can choose. The only real drawback to Ethernet is the need to run wires between all the computers that will participate in the network and the hub or switch that is used to connect the computers to each other. Ethernet wires are referred to as *Category 5* (CAT5 or CAT5e) cables and have been specified as a standard by Electronics Industries Alliance (EIA) /Telecommunications Industry Association (TIA). (CAT5 is also known as the EIA/TIA 568 standard.) If you're interested in more detail, you can visit http://wikipedia.org and search for Category 5 cable or EIA/TIA.

Choosing Your Ethernet Cables

Various cable types can be used to connect computers to each other with varying speeds. CAT5 cables are designed to provide reliable data communications for Ethernet networks up to 100Mbps. The maximum distance that data can be transmitted reliably with a CAT5 cable is 100 meters, or just about 330 feet. CAT5e cables are designed to provide reliable data communications for Ethernet networks up 1000Mbps (referred to as *Gigabit Ethernet*). The

OTHER TYPES OF NETWORKING

While Ethernet is king in terms of networking these days, it was not always so. Much the same as the battle between the Sony Beta and the JVC VHS video recorder formats. In years past Ethernet was considered inferior to a technology introduced by IBM called Token Ring. Before Token Ring, there was ARCNET which was developed by Datapoint Corporation. The feature that endeared the Token Ring and ARCNET to the geeks of the time was their deterministic nature. There was a very orderly process and each computer on the network was guaranteed a time when it could transmit. Until a computer had the floor (so to speak) all it could do was listen. This guaranteed that there would be no traffic jams since only one computer could transmit at a time. Ethernet by contrast is what is called a multiple access medium and is prone to communications collisions. It is this nature that requires Ethernet to create a way to detect when multiple computers have attempted a transmission, detect the condition, and recover from it.

maximum distance that data can be transmitted reliably with a CAT5e cable is 100 meters, assuming a gigabit network. CAT5e cables can also be used in 100Mbps Ethernet networks, where the advantage they offer is a maximum distance of 350 meters, as opposed to 100 meters offered by CAT5 cables.

NOTE

You might want to be aware of the CAT3 standard, although chances are that you will have little need for it from this point on. The CAT3 specification defines a cable that is used for data transmission on 10Mbps networks over a maximum distance of 100 meters. EIA and TIA are the organizations responsible for these standards.

A central device called the *hub* or *switch* is used as the communications command center for each computer. The difference between a hub and switch has to do with whether the speed of the connection is shared or dedicated to a single computer:

▶ A *hub* shares the bandwidth of the connection among all the computers connected to it. For example, if you have five computers connected to a 10Mbps hub, they are all sharing that 10Mbps bandwidth. What's more, all those computers contend with each other for access to the medium because the rules of the Ethernet protocol define only one sender at a time.

▶ A *switch* provides dedicated bandwidth to each computer connected to it. The advantage is that a switch doesn't impose the limitation of a single computer transmitting at one time. Each computer is able to utilize the full bandwidth available, without concern for whether any of the other computers are transmitting data.

The original Ethernet specification was intended to be implemented by using a hub and a data transmission rate of 10Mbps. CAT3 cables were used back then. The 100Mbps Ethernet implementation is called Fast Ethernet, and, as we have already discussed, it is intended to be run over CAT5 cables. Chances are that if you have a recent computer, you will only need to concern yourself with Fast Ethernet and possibly Gigabit Ethernet speeds. This makes your choice a lot easier in terms of hub or switch selection. While it is possible to buy a Fast Ethernet hub, it really makes no practical or financial sense to do so. The speed difference you gain is worth the nominal price increase you will pay for a switch versus a hub.

The single greatest factor influencing your home networking decision may rest on where your computers will be located and/or whether your home is already wired for computer networking. You may also want to consider running wires behind walls yourself or having them run for you by a qualified technician. These latter two options can be either time-consuming or costly, depending on the number of computers and difficulty running the wires. If all your computers will be located in a single room, wired Ethernet may be the most economical choice. If, however, your computers consist of laptops that will move from room to room, you might want to consider wireless networking as an alternative.

Wireless Networking

If your home network is not contained within a single room, or if wiring is not a viable option for you, then one of the available wireless networking solutions is the way to go. The drawbacks to wireless networking are that the cost is somewhat higher than that of wired Ethernet solutions and that the configuration can be a bit more time-consuming. Security is also a concern with wireless networks. Keep in mind that your data is traveling across radio frequencies, which are available to anyone with the right equipment to receive those signals.

Wireless Networking Hardware

To create a wireless home network, you need to consider two types of hardware: a WAP and network interface cards (NICs).

WAPs

For any type of wireless network, you need to purchase a wireless access point (WAP). WAPs, which are the wireless equivalent of hubs and switches in a wired environment, come in many different varieties. You need to consider whether to buy a WAP that also includes routing features (very common these days), which is a great benefit when you're connecting a home network to the Internet through an ISP. One of the great benefits of WAPs these days is that you can simply plug them in to your ISP connection and then make simple configurations on your home computers to enable networking. Because of this ease of use, the projects in this book implement wireless networking.

WAPs vary in their capabilities, and you will certainly want to read the manual for the WAP that you choose for your network. In general, you should look for what is called a *wireless router*, which you can usually buy for less than $100. A wireless router includes WAP functionality along with an Ethernet switch that accommodates speeds of 10Mbps and 100Mbps, usually with four ports, and a separate connection for linking to your ISP connection.

Wireless NICs

To build a wireless network, you also need a wireless NIC for each of your computers. Each notebook or laptop type of device needs a PC card device or a USB wireless NIC, and each desktop can use either an internally installed NIC or a USB wireless NIC. Wireless NICs are fairly inexpensive; you can buy most for less than $50, and there are quite a few you can buy for around $25. Many manufacturers of both laptops and desktops include NICs in their systems. So you may not have to purchase one when you decide to put together your network.

NOTE

USB NICs are a bit slower than built-in NICs.

Wireless Networking Standards

When people talk about wireless networking, they are referring to what is commonly known as the 802.11 standard, which is specified by the Institute of Electrical and Electronics Engineers (IEEE). You can obtain exhaustive

WHERE DO THE STANDARDS COME FROM?

The computer networking industry is rich with standards that have been developed over the years. Sometimes the sheer volume of available standards can be overwhelming especially when you are trying to figure out what you need for your network and the salesperson at Computer City, Radio Shack, Best Buy, Fry's, or the local computer shop keeps tossing acronyms left and right that you're not sure of. You can and should educate yourself a bit before jumping into the fray. Online articles are available to cover all of the standards you will ever encounter. You should be particularly aware of the IEEE (Institute of Electrical and Electronics Engineers) and EIA/TIA (Electronics and Telecommunications Industries Associations). The IEEE is generally concerned with specifications dealing with things like the Ethernet wired and wireless communications standards rather than the physical medium upon which communications will take place. The EIA/TIA organizations on the other hand are concerned with the standards that define things like the cable and connectors used to enable computer communications. So with a bit of research you will have some background into things like the 802.3 standard and what an RJ-11 or RJ-45 is as well as why you would need them.

information on the various 802.11 wireless specifications from the IEEE website, at http://standards.ieee.org/wireless. As with many things relating to computers and networking, it is important to understand the terminology related to wireless networking. The following sections describe the three most common 802.11 standards: 802.11b, 802.11a, and 802.11g.

The 802.11b Wireless Standard

The first 802.11 standard to be implemented was 802.11b. The data communications speed expectation of 802.11b is 11Mbps; however, the actual speed is influenced by the amount of interference the signal encounters. 802.11b wireless networks operate on a radio frequency of 2.4 Gigahertz (GHz), so you will often have problems in such networks if you have cordless phones that share this frequency. You can solve this problem by either moving your wireless equipment as far from your cordless device as possible, by using 900MHz or 5.8GHz phones, or by opting for another of the wireless standards.

The 802.11a Wireless Standard

802.11a is a bit odd in the lexicon of wireless networking history. It is an upgrade to the 802.11b technology, even though sequentially you would think it was the first to be released. However, it is a mutually exclusive upgrade in that you can't run both 802.11b and 802.11a on the same network. The advantage offered by 802.11a is speed; it is capable of data transmission at 54Mbps, which is a five-fold increase over the speed offered by 802.11b. WAPs and NICs in the 802.11a environment also operate on radio frequency technology, but they work in the 5GHz range, so interference with cordless phones is a problem only if you use 5.8GHz phones.

The 802.11g Wireless Standard

802.11g offers a true upgrade over the other wireless standards in that you can mix 802.11b devices with 802.11g devices. As with the 802.11a standard, speed is the primary reason for moving to 802.11g, where data is transmitted at 54Mbps. The advantage of moving from 802.11b to 802.11g, of course, is that you are not required to perform a wholesale upgrade of all devices on the network. The most important consideration is that your WAP can accommodate the fastest wireless NIC on the network. So by installing an 802.11g WAP, you are able to mix the NICs in your computers. The 802.11b devices will be able to transmit at 11Mbps, and the 802.11g devices will be able to transmit at 54Mbps, all on the same network. 802.11g devices operate on the 2.4GHz frequency, so your wireless interference issues are the same as with 802.11b devices. You will likely only encounter 802.11g wireless networking if you control the creation of your wireless network. If some of your computer equipment is a little older, you may have to make provisions for slower-speed devices.

Choosing a Network Type

So far in this chapter, we have covered wired Ethernet solutions and what you can expect by creating and using one. We have also covered wireless solutions and what you can expect by choosing one of them. Table 2.1 summarizes the various technologies we have discussed.

TABLE 2.1   Comparison of Available Networking Solutions

Technology	Speed	Wireless
Ethernet 10	10Mbps	No
Ethernet 100	100Mbps	No
Gigabit Ethernet	1000Mbps	No
802.11b	11Mbps	Yes
802.11a	54Mbps	Yes
802.11g	54Mbps	Yes

Ease-of-use and installation are usually the prime decision-making factors in setting up a home network, so this book shows how to implement a wireless network. Specifically, it shows how to use 802.11g devices.

Remember that laptops can use PC card or USB NICs, while desktop computers use USB NICs for wireless networking. So the first order of business in setting up your network is getting everything set up so that your computers can communicate. At this point we will start delving into our projects, which detail the steps required to configure the computers in your home network. In these projects, you will connect your home network to the Internet through a wireless router. You will plug this device in to your ISP connection through a port designated for your Internet connection. (You need to refer to your manufacturer's instructions for specific details on how to do this.) It is important that you place the wireless router as close to the middle of your home network as possible, and you need to place it as high as you can.

Because you are using a wireless networking solution, you will need to be sure that you understand the security implications. If you set up your wireless router by plugging it in directly out of the box, it will certainly work. However, with that configuration, your network is available to anyone who has a wireless networking device and happens to be within range of your wireless signal. While this may not seem to be a big problem, you need to realize that this means that people may have access to your network, which means the information on your computers is vulnerable to attack.

You have a couple choices when looking at wireless security: Wired Equivalent Privacy (WEP) and Wi-Fi Protected Access (WPA). WEP provides you with a modicum of security, and it is fairly easy to break for someone who really wants to get into your wireless network. Using WEP is somewhat like locking your windows: Someone will be less likely to try tampering with your WEP-protected network than with one with no protection whatsoever. WPA is really the state-of-the-art as far as wireless security is concerned. The steps outlined in this book show you how to configure your network for WEP security as a compatibility precaution. Some wireless network cards do not support WPA, so you should check your equipment. For detailed background information on WPA, refer to www.wi-fi.org.

As background for the projects in this book, you should read the manual that came with your wireless router to ensure that you have configured it in the fashion recommended by the manufacturer.

Configuring Your Computers for Wireless Access

The following sections walk through how to configure your computers for wireless access. In this solution, you will install a wireless router that is connected to your ISP link. You will enable WEP, and you will have to enter a key in order to be able to access the wireless network. You will learn how to configure your computers so that they can communicate with each other on your wireless network.

To configure your computers for wireless networking, follow these steps:

1. Select Start, Control Panel and then double-click Network Connections. The Network Connections page appears (see Figure 2.1).

2. On the Network Connections page, right-click your wireless network connection and then click Properties.

3. On the Wireless Network Connection Properties page, select the Wireless Networks tab (see Figure 2.2) and then click Properties.

NOTE

If your wireless network does not appear under Preferred Networks, click View Wireless Networks. If your network still does not appear, click Refresh Network List, select your wireless network from the list, and then click Change Advanced Settings. At this point, retry step 3. If your network name still does not appear, review the instructions that came with your network devices to ensure that you have configured the equipment as required.

FIGURE 2.1
**The Network
Connections page.**

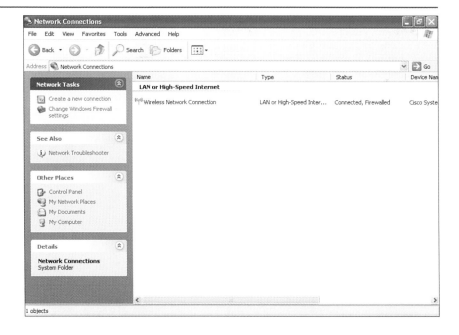

FIGURE 2.2
The Wireless Network Connection Properties page.

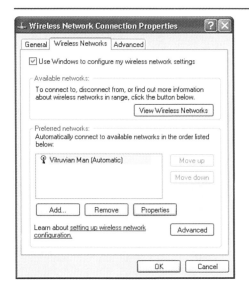

4. Complete the page as follows:

   ▸ Set Network Authentication to Open.

   ▸ Set Data Encryption to WEP.

   ▸ Set Network Key to the key entered when the wireless router was configured for WEP.

   When you are done with these settings, click OK twice and close the Network Connections page.

If you choose to use WPA security in your wireless network, you need to read the Microsoft Knowledge Base article on WPA support for Windows XP, at http://support.microsoft.com/?kbid=815485.

Testing Your Computers' Connectivity

At this point, your computers should be able to communicate with each other. To verify that they can, try the following connectivity test:

1. Select Start, Run, type **CMD**, and then click OK.

2. In the command window, type **ipconfig /all** and then press Enter.

3. Note the default gateway and DHCP server IP addresses.

4. Type **ping *w.x.y.z***, where *w.x.y.z* is the IP addresses noted in step 3. You also need to use the IP address of another computer on your network. You should see four almost-identical lines, starting with Reply from *w.x.y.z....*

> **NOTE**
>
> **If you are having trouble establishing a connection at this point, you should refer to the troubleshooting topics in Chapter 7, "When Your Network Doesn't Work the Way It Should."**

You have now confirmed that your home network computers have basic connectivity.

Testing Your Internet Connectivity

You need to make sure that your computers can access the Internet. To verify this, follow these steps:

1. Open your web browser by selecting Start, Internet Explorer. You should see a web page displayed on your screen at this point.

2. If you have trouble seeing an Internet page, verify your ISP link by contacting to your ISP's technical support group. (Because the variety of Internet connections is wide, it is beyond the scope of this book to cover troubleshooting of every type of problem.)

Summary

This chapter expands your basic knowledge for home networking. You have seen the various solutions available and walked through how to configure your computers to get them communicating with each other. Chapter 3, "Project 2: Sharing Files, Printers, and Other Stuff on Your Network," looks at how to start sharing things between your computers. Now that you have a good foundation for your network, it will be up and running very shortly.

Project 2: Sharing Files, Printers, and Other Stuff on Your Network

Now that your computers are communicating, you can turn to the task of starting to do something useful with them. In Chapter 2, "Project 1: Making Your Computers Talk to Each Other," you went through your first project. In this and subsequent chapters you will continue to take the steps required for particular solutions. This chapter looks at how to share files, printers, and other devices among the computers in your home network.

Running the Network Setup Wizard

To get your home network ready to share information and equipment, you need to run the Network Setup Wizard once on each computer in the network. Before you work through the following steps, you should think about the names you want to assign to your network and to each computer. A short, descriptive name for the network, such as HOME, works well. Your computer names should indicate to whom the computer belongs or where it is located, such as BEDROOM or KITCHEN. If you use descriptive names, when you are looking for information and as your home network grows, it will be easier for you to identify which computer you are connecting to.

To run the Network Setup Wizard, follow these steps:

1. Select Start, Control Panel. The Control Panel opens.

2. If your page title is Pick a Category, select Network and Internet Connections (see Figure 3.1). The Pick a Task window appears.

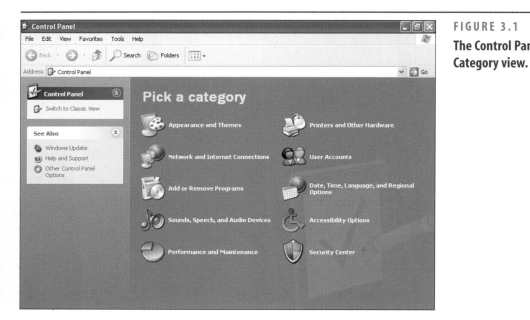

FIGURE 3.1

The Control Panel in Category view.

3. Select Network Connections from either the screen shown in Figure 3.2 (if your Control Panel is in Category view) or the one shown in Figure 3.3 (if your Control Panel is in Classic view). The Network Connections window appears (see Figure 3.4).

FIGURE 3.2

The Control Panel in Category view.

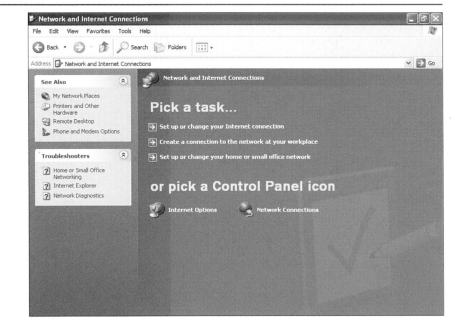

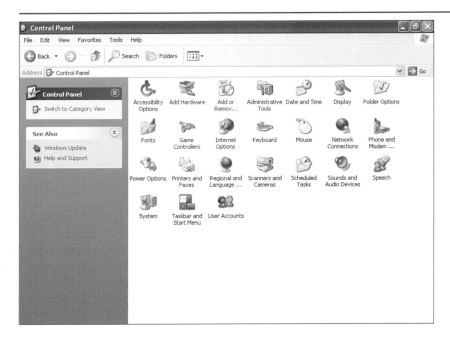

FIGURE 3.3

The Control Panel in Classic view.

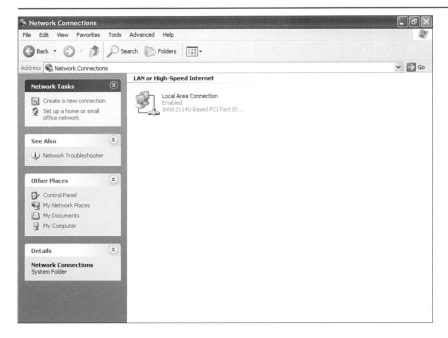

FIGURE 3.4

The Network Connections window.

4. Click Set Up a Home or Small Office Network. The Welcome to the Network Setup Wizard page appears (see Figure 3.5).

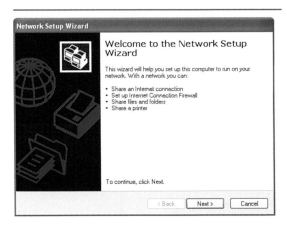

FIGURE 3.5
The Network Setup Wizard.

5. Click Next. The Before You Continue page appears.

6. Click Next. The Select a Connection Method page appears (see Figure 3.6).

7. Ensure that the option This Computer Connects to the Internet Through Another Computer on My Network or Through a Residential Gateway is selected and then click Next. The Give This Computer a Description and Name page appears (see Figure 3.7)

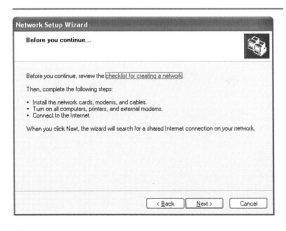

FIGURE 3.6
The Select a Connection Method page.

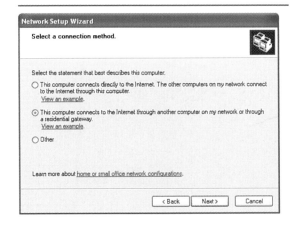

FIGURE 3.7
The Give This Computer a Description and Name page.

8. Enter descriptive information for this computer and then click Next. The computers in this example use the names BEDROOM and FAMILYROOM. The Name Your Network page appears (see Figure 3.8).

WINDOWS NETWORKING

Windows XP can be networked in one of two modes: workgroup or domain networking.

In workgroup networks, Windows computers participate in a so-called workgroup for ease of connectivity. It is possible for a physical network to consist of more than one workgroup. Imagine a business setting with multiple departments, where it would be advantageous to primarily see the computers in your immediate department but yet have the ability to see your colleagues' computers in other departments at the same time. This is what workgroup networking offers.

With domain-based networking, you install a central server called the *domain controller*. This computer acts as the central repository for all logon identities used on the network and allows everyone on the network to see the other computers that are connected. In addition to providing centralized user accounts, you can use domain-based networking to maintain a standard desktop profile as well as enforce security settings from a centralized location, among many other benefits. For more information on domain-based networking, you can check Microsoft's website.

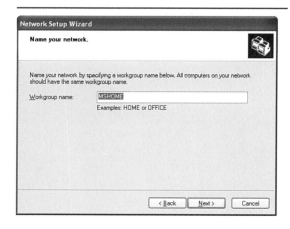

FIGURE 3.8

The Name Your Network page.

9. Enter a short description for your network and then click Next. This example uses the default workgroup name MSHOME. The Ready to Apply Network Settings page appears.

10. Click Next. The You're Almost Done page appears.

11. Select Just Finish the Wizard; I Don't Need to Run the Wizard on Other Computers. The Completing the Network Setup Wizard page appears (see Figure 3.9).

12. Click Finish.

13. Click Yes when you're prompted to restart your computer.

FIGURE 3.9
The Completing the Network Setup Wizard page.

Sharing Files on Your Home Network

This section walks your through how to share files on your network. The scenario you work with in this section assumes that you have one computer on which your family photographs are stored, and you would like to be able to get to the photos from any computer on the network. In the end, you will be able to not only view these photographs from any computer, but you will be able to edit them as well, assuming that you have the appropriate photo editing software. In your home network, you will be working on the BEDROOM computer, accessing photographs on the FAMI-LYROOM computer. If you have a digital camera, you will want to read the sidebar on how to transfer your photos from your digital camera to your computer.

To share photos on your home network, follow these steps:

1. On the FAMILYROOM computer, select Start, My Computer. The screen shown in Figure 3.10 appears.

NOTE

If you do not see the My Computer menu item, you need to right-click the Start menu and then click Properties. You then see the Taskbar and Start Menu Properties page. On the Start Menu tab, click Customize and then click Advanced. Scroll through the Start menu items until you come to the entry for My Computer. Ensure that this option is set to something other than Don't Display This Item.

NOTE

You'll notice that under Files Stored on This Computer, the Shared Documents folder shows a hand underneath the folder name. This indicates that the folder is being shared. The Shared Documents folder is intended to be a location where files can be placed and shared by all users of a particular computer. When you run the Network Setup Wizard, this folder automatically becomes shared. You can also use the Shared Documents folder as a repository for the items you want to share with other computers on your network, but that would involve copying files between folders on your computer. You can do that instead by sharing individual folders.

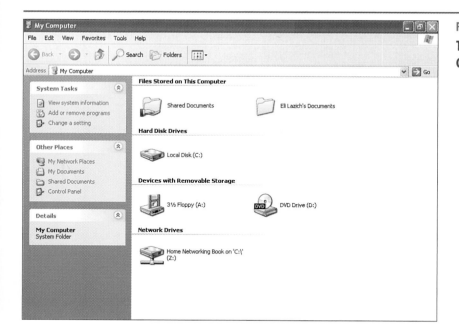

FIGURE 3.10

The contents of My Computer.

2. Under Other Places, select My Documents.

3. Right-click the My Pictures folder and then click Sharing and Security. The My Pictures Properties page appears.

4. Select Share This Folder on the Network and then click OK.

NOTE

Notice that the My Pictures folder displays a hand underneath it, indicating that it is now being shared. For this scenario to work as expected, you need to double-click the Sample Pictures folder and then select Edit, Select All. You then need to click the Back button to move up to the My Pictures folder once again and then select Edit, Paste. The pictures then appear in the proper place for this exercise.

Accessing Shared Files on Your Home Network

You need to move to your BEDROOM computer for the next section. From there, you can access the photographs on the FAMILYROOM computer by following these steps:

1. On the BEDROOM computer, select Start, My Computer.

2. Under Other Places, click My Network Places. The window shown in Figure 3.11 appears.

FIGURE 3.11

The My Network Places window.

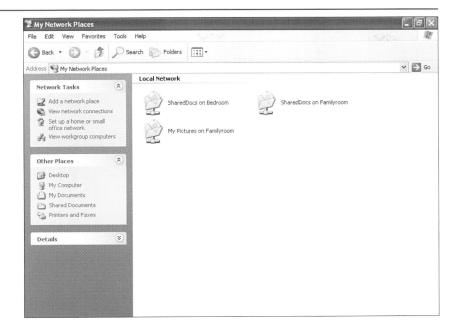

3. Double-click My Pictures on Familyroom and then double-click one of the pictures you see listed. You are now placed into a viewer from which you can move forward or backward through the photographs on the FAMILYROOM computer. If you have photo editing software, such as Adobe's Photoshop, you can edit your pictures, create projects such as greeting cards with your pictures, and print the results.

Sharing Printers on Your Home Network

In the following sections, you will share the printer attached to the FAMILYROOM computer. You will then be able to print

documents from the BEDROOM computer. This will save you the trouble of having to walk down to the FAMILYROOM computer with your files in order to print them.

In this example, you will install a generic printer. Keep in mind that your printer installation may differ from what you see here, depending on the printer. This example is meant to show you the basics of verifying networking printing capabilities. Installing a printer in Windows XP is a fairly straightforward task; Windows XP guides you through the entire process unless you have a very unusual printer model. In that case, you should follow your manufacturer's directions for installing the printer.

Try editing one of the pictures on the remote computer (that is, the FAMILYROOM computer) by right-clicking the picture and then clicking Edit. This starts the Paint application, which you can use to draw on the existing picture. After you draw a few lines, select File, Save As and then give your new picture a name. Because sharing is configured to only allow read access and not the ability to change files by default, your changes will not be saved.

Now go back to the FAMILYROOM computer, right-click the My Pictures folder that is being shared, and then click Sharing and Security. Now click Allow Network Users to Change My Files and try to edit another picture, following the preceding procedure. You should now be able to save your changes.

Using this method is a way to share your files yet maintain security. Your family members can see your photographs in this case, but they cannot make changes to them.

Sharing Your Printer

To share your printer with the rest of the computers in your home network, follow these steps:

1. Select Start, Printers and Faxes. The window shown in Figure 3.12 appears.

2. Right-click the printer you want to share and then click Sharing.

3. On the Properties page for the printer, select Share This Printer and then click OK.

Connecting To and Using a Shared Printer

At this point you will connect to the shared printer from the preceding section. After you make the connection, you will send a file to the printer. You will use the Notepad application in this project to verify printing capabilities. However, you could use any other Windows application to do this by selecting File Print. Then you follow the onscreen instructions to print your document, which is usually as easy as a click on the OK or Print buttons.

To connect to a shared printer on your home network, follow these steps:

1. Select Start, Printers and Faxes.

2. Under Printer Tasks, select Add a Printer. The Welcome to the Add Printer Wizard page appears.

3. Click Next. The Local or Network Printer page appears (see Figure 3.13).

FIGURE 3.12

The Printers and Faxes window.

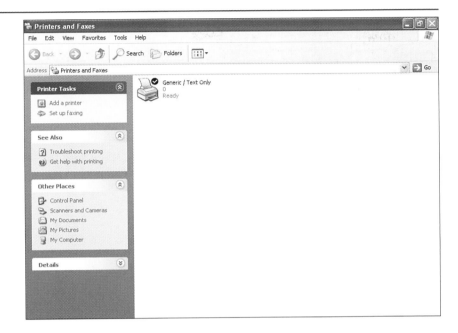

FIGURE 3.13

The Local or Network Printer page.

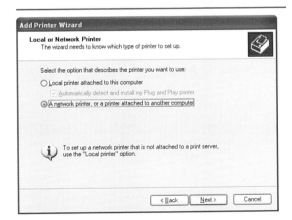

4. Select the option A Network Printer, or a Printer Attached to Another Computer and then click Next.

5. You may have to double-click the computer on which the printer is located and then select the printer, click Next, and then click Finish to complete the wizard. The printer is now installed.

6. Select Start, All Programs, Accessories, Notepad. The Notepad application opens.

7. In Notepad, type some text onscreen then select File, Print.

8. If you see the Print dialog box, choose your printer and then click Print.

Summary

At this point, you have enabled your home network to share files and printers. You have also tried sharing your photographs with the rest of your family members. You can now print your photographs, homework, tax forms, meal recipes, or any other documents to the family printer located in the family room. You are well on your way to creating an efficient networking environment for your home.

Project 3: Creating a Network Jukebox

iTunes is software that lets you organize and listen to your music and other audio files on your computer, using the audio hardware in your computer. The following are some of the things you can do with iTunes:

- ▶ **Listen to CDs**—Listening to music with iTunes is as easy as putting a CD into your computer and clicking Play. When you insert a CD, iTunes starts, and the CD appears in the Source list.

- ▶ **Add music from CDs or from the Internet to your iTunes library**—After you import music to your library, you can play it, transfer it to your MP3 player, edit the song information, and more. To listen to a song, you double-click it in your library.

- ▶ **Buy songs from the iTunes Music Store**—You can even have the music automatically downloaded to your hard disk and imported into your library.

- ▶ **Create lists of your favorite songs**—iTunes lets you organize your music into playlists. You can create playlists to suit a specific need, such as a party mix.

- ▶ **Transfer music to your MP3 player**—If you have an MP3 player, you can set it to update automatically with songs from your music library.

- ▶ **Make your own CDs or DVDs**—You can use iTunes to make your own custom discs containing songs in a playlist.

- ▶ **Subscribe to and listen to podcasts**—Podcasts are downloadable short-length shows delivered by iTunes.

continues

CHAPTER 4   PROJECT 3: CREATING A NETWORK JUKEBOX

This chapter looks at networking as it relates to entertainment—specifically, music. You will see what it takes to create a collection of music on the various computers in your home network and then learn how to access that music from any computer.

Imagine that you have a collection of CDs from various eras and genres that the people in your house listen to. Mom and Dad might want to hear the oldies, while the kids want to hear the latest CDs they've bought recently. You can obviously play these CDs on your stereo equipment, but as computers are becoming more prevalent and the audio hardware included is of continually better quality, you can just as easily and privately play them on your own computer.

Installing iTunes

The example in this chapter involves using the iTunes software, which is available from www.itunes.com. iTunes gives you the capability to not only create a virtual jukebox but also purchase your favorite music online, create customized playlists, and even burn your own music CDs to enjoy in your car or stereo. You can even use iTunes to transfer your music collection to your portable music player, such as an iPod device or other MP3 player. When I was a kid, I wrote a notebook to inventory my growing music collection, and I included notes about which were my favorite tracks. With iTunes, you can catalog all this information electronically so that you'll know at a glance which songs you consider to be better than others. To begin, we will look at how to obtain and install the latest version of the iTunes software for your network.

You can get a copy of the iTunes software from the iTunes website at www.itunes.com. Follow the instructions on the site to download a copy of the software to your local computer. Then follow these steps to install iTunes:

1. On your local hard disk, go to the folder where you saved the iTunes download.

2. Double-click **iTunesSetup.exe**. If you see the Open File—Security Warning dialog box, click Run. If you do not see the Warning dialog box, the Welcome to the iTunes 4 Installer page appears (see Figure 4.1).

▶ **Share your music library across computers—Music sharing lets you stream your library across a local network so you can listen to your music on multiple computers without having to import it into iTunes on each computer.**

▶ **Listen to Internet radio stations—Internet radio stations broadcast music that you can listen to with iTunes.**

FIGURE 4.1
The Welcome to the iTunes 4 Installer page.

3. Click Next. The License Agreement page appears.

4. Click Yes. The Information page appears.

5. Click Next. The Setup Type page appears.

6. Click Next. The Choose Destination Location page appears.

7. Click Next. The Enjoy Your iTunes Music Anywhere page appears.

8. Click Next. The Installation Successful page appears.

9. Click Finish to finish the installation process.

Working with iTunes

Now that you have iTunes installed, you can configure it to suit your preferences. Notice that the installation has placed the iTunes and QuickTime player icons (assuming that you accepted the default options) on your desktop.

To configure iTunes, follow these steps:

1. Double-click the iTunes icon on your desktop. The iTunes software opens, and the first screen you see is the license agreement screen.

2. Read the license agreement, and if you accept it, click Agree. The Welcome to iTunes page appears.

3. Click Next. The Find Music Files page appears.

4. Click Next. The Keep iTunes Music Folder Organized page appears.

NOTE

Clicking Next on the Find Music Files page causes iTunes to search your hard disk for any music files and add them to the iTunes library. You can choose to do this later if you would rather manually add music to your iTunes library. Keep in mind that the library is just that: the repository of all music contained on the computer. Just as you might have sorted your physical music collection, you will have the ability to sort your virtual music collection. You should be aware that if you have music in the Windows Media Player Windows Media Audio (WMA) format, iTunes will make a copy of the file and import it using your preferences, which will likely be the AAC file format. This has the potential to use a large amount of disk space on your computer. Protected WMA files cannot be added to iTunes.

5. Click Next. The iTunes Music Store page appears.

NOTE

Be careful with the Keep iTunes Music Folder Organized page. As the text onscreen tells you, if you change anything about a song file's name, iTunes will automatically reorganize your music. I prefer to control my music libraries, so I stay with the default setting here.

6. Click No, Take Me to My iTunes library. The iTunes library appears.

NOTE

This process could take some time if you have a lot of music on your computer. You might want to see if there is any other music you want to add to iTunes in your CD collection while this is taking place.

Using the iTunes Library

The iTunes library shows you all the music you have obtained from CDs, the Internet, and other sources, such as the iTunes Music Store. (As shown in Figure 4.2, you can find the iTunes Music Store in the Source window on the left side of the iTunes interface.)

You can play the music listed in your library on the computer where you are running iTunes either directly from the library sequentially or randomly, or you can create custom playlists from which to play your music. You can also transfer music from your library to a portable music player. If you want to burn a CD filled with your favorite music, you need to create a playlist before creating your CD.

Adding Music to Your Library

As mentioned previously, there are a number of ways to obtain music to add to your library. The method we will look at here is adding music from your own personal CD collection. The process of copying music from an audio CD to your computer is often referred to as "ripping." Keep in mind that you can also choose to buy music on the Internet by using the iTunes Music Store.

MORE ABOUT MUSIC FILES

iTunes stores music in the MPEG-4 Advanced Audio Coding (AAC) format by default. You have a choice when importing music from original media (such as CDs you own) as to which format they will be stored in. AAC is a wide-band coding method that you should use as your preferred method of importing because the amount of data storage required for songs at high fidelity is lower than with previous MPEG standards. You also have the choice to import your songs in the MPEG-3 (MP3) and WMA formats. The reasons for choosing these formats vary; for example, if your WMA files are protected, you will not be able to convert them to AAC files. If you have a portable media player that is not compatible with AAC-encoded files, you will have to use either MP3 or WMA, depending on which is supported by your player.

FIGURE 4.2

The iTunes Source window.

To add music from your CDs to your iTunes library, follow these steps:

1. With iTunes running, insert a CD into the CD drive and close the tray. After a brief delay, the songs on the CD are listed in the iTunes interface (see Figure 4.3).

2. Ensure that the check box is clear for any song you do not want to record.

3. To add the songs to your iTunes library, click the Import icon in the upper-right corner of the iTunes interface.

4. When all the songs have been transferred, you can eject the disc by clicking the Eject icon to the right of the CD title in the iTunes interface.

NOTE

iTunes automatically begins to play songs while you are importing them from the CD. To change this behavior, you can either click the Pause button or you can select Edit, Preferences, select the Importing tab, and then clear the check box next to Play Songs While Importing. This disables playback for all future import sessions.

After you eject your CD, you can find the music you imported in the library by sorting on one of the available columns. To sort by any column heading, you click the column name. To reverse the sort, you click the column name a second time.

FIGURE 4.3
An iTunes CD track listing.

Sharing Music by Using iTunes

After you import files, you will inevitably want to share them with others in your home network. After all, the whole point here is to create a jukebox repository that everyone can enjoy from his or her own computer. The advantage this offers to the home network is the ability to either have all your music stored in one central location or distributed across two or more computers, yet still be accessible from anywhere. You could, for example, take your laptop with you anywhere you travel, and when you return home, you'll still be able to play all your favorite songs. Therefore, you'll now learn how to share music.

To share music by using iTunes, follow these steps:

1. In the iTunes interface, select Edit, Preferences.

2. Select the Sharing tab and then select the Share My Music check box (see Figure 4.4).

FIGURE 4.4
The iTunes Sharing tab.

> **NOTE**
>
> You can choose to share your entire library or selected playlists. You can also choose a name for your shared music, and you can even require a password so that if you want only certain people on the network to access particular pieces of music, you can do so.
>
> Note that if you choose to share playlists, the remote computer does not see the playlist name but rather sees all the songs on the combined playlists.

3. Click OK to accept the defaults and then click OK on the reminder page.

Accessing Shared Music

Now that you have enabled shared music, it's time to take a look at how to access your music from a remote machine. Say you are in your bedroom and would like to access a collection of music on your FAMILYROOM computer. You just bought a new sound system for your bedroom and have connected to your laptop's audio output to your stereo and want to test your new setup. Here's what you do:

1. Ensure that the FAMILYROOM computer is turned on so that you can access your shared music.

2. Start iTunes on the bedroom computer. An additional item appears under the Source section of the screen. You also see a similar listing for each computer that has enabled sharing. So if you have six computers in your home network and all of them share music, you should expect to see a share listing for five computers in addition to the local library for your computer (see Figure 4.5).

The Eli Lazich's Music item in Figure 4.5 appears as a result of enabling shared music on the family room computer. To play any of the songs listed in the shared music folder, select a song and then click Play in the upper-left portion of the screen.

FIGURE 4.5
Accessing shared music.

Creating and Using Playlists

While the library contains all the imported music contained on your computer, you may not want to browse through every song to get to one that you want to hear. This is where playlists come in very handy. You can create a playlist to suit just about any occasion, including theme parties, weddings, sporting events, and graduations. Playlists are tied to the computer on whose library the music exists. This means that if you are accessing music by using the shared music feature, you cannot access playlists on the remote computer. In the following section you will create a playlist that is geared toward Christmas music for a holiday party. In this example, you'll play the songs from a Christmas album released by Chris Isaak during the 2004 holiday season as shown in Figure 4.6.

Creating a Playlist

To create a playlist in iTunes, follow these steps:

1. In the iTunes interface, select File, New Playlist, type a name for your playlist, and then press Enter.

2. Click the first song you want to include in your playlist and then hold down the Ctrl key while you click each additional song you want to add to the playlist. The order in which you select songs doesn't matter; you can rearrange the playing order after you create the playlist.

3. Move your mouse icon over any of the songs to be included in the playlist and then click and hold your left mouse button. While holding the left mouse button, drag your mouse over the playlist you created and release the button.

FIGURE 4.6
Creating a playlist.

4. Click the playlist you created in step 1. You should now see the songs you chose listed.

What You Can Do with Playlists

After you have created a playlist, if you right-click the playlist name in the iTunes interface, you see that you can burn the contents of this playlist to a CD. Burning to a CD requires that you have a CD burner and the appropriate writable CD media. You can set your burning preferences by selecting Edit, Preferences and then selecting the Burning tab (see Figure 4.7). This tab provides a few options for creating your own CDs:

▶ **Create an Audio CD**—This option creates a CD that is compatible with most home, car, and portable CD players. You can expect about 20 songs per CD, at the most, in this mode. Each CD shows the recording capacity on its label, and you can use that as a guide to how many songs will fit on a CD.

▶ **Create an MP3 CD**—This option creates a disc containing the digitally encoded music files you choose. Music compresses very well in digital format, and you can expect a great deal more music to fit on a CD when stored in MP3 format than when in audio CD format. Consider that at high audio quality, a 4-minute song in MP3 format requires about 4MB of storage. Using simple math, you can see that somewhere in the neighborhood of 150 or more songs of this size will fit on a single CD. This gives you about 10 hours of music on a single CD. The catch (there's always a catch) is that your equipment must be capable of playing MP3-formatted media. Most new CD players for the home and car are capable of this, but you'll certainly want to check to make sure before creating a disc full of MP3 content.

FIGURE 4.7

CD burning options.

▶ **Create a backup CD or DVD**—This option transfers your digitally encoded music files to either a CD or DVD disc. The approach is the same as that for creating an audio CD: Create a playlist, right-click, and choose the Burn to Disc option. The biggest attraction here is that you can take advantage of the greater capacity offered by storing your music on a DVD rather than a CD.

To choose a disc burning option, you click Edit, Preferences. On the Burning tab in the Preferences window, you choose your preferred disc format. Then you can begin the disc burning process.

Summary

By now, you know how to transfer music from your CD collection to your computer. You also know how to share your music throughout your home network, and you can even burn your own customized CDs for enjoyment on your home or car CD player. A number of features are available in iTunes that can add to the major functionality described in this chapter. For example, you can customize the listening experience to get the best possible sound for your setting. If your library gets too large to search manually, you can refine your searches in iTunes to find exactly the music you are looking for. You can find this and much more helpful information in the iTunes online help system, which you can access by selecting the Help drop-down menu.

SMART PLAYLISTS

Playlists give you the flexibility of arranging your music according to your own needs. A feature that bears mentioning here is the Smart Playlist. With it, you can have iTunes create playlists for you by providing key pieces of information about the types of songs you want to include. For example, a smart playlist could contain all songs from a particular artist, or songs that contain a certain word or phrase. You can create smart playlists by selecting File, New Smart Playlist.

For now, you can sit back, relax, and enjoy some of your music. You don't even need to get up to change discs once you get everything on your computer network. Start thinking of the ways in which you can be your very own domestic DJ.

Project 4: Instant Messaging in and out of Your Home Network

IM is offered by a variety of services. America Online (AOL) offers what it calls the AOL Instant Messenger (AIM), Yahoo offers Yahoo Messenger, ICQ offers a messenger that was in fact the first available IM client, and MSN offers its own MSN Messenger. What they all have in common is the basic functionality that IM provides to users, which is the ability to carry on conversations across a network connection.

The way these messenger services work is that you sign up with the provider, and your contact information is stored by and specific to that provider. Your IM client makes a connection to your provider's server to obtain information about your contacts. This all works well when you want to contact someone who happens to be a user of the same service you are using, but you encounter issues when attempting to communicate with users of other providers' solutions. For example, MSN's Messenger is compatible with the Windows Messenger already installed on your computer, but you will encounter problems if you attempt to add people from AOL, Yahoo, or ICQ to your contact list and start conversations with them.

As a user, you need a tool to bridge the gap, and one such tool is called Trillian. A quick search on Google should turn up enough information to get you started with Trillian. The basic premise behind Trillian is that it enables you to communicate with users of IM clients from other providers.

CHAPTER 5 PROJECT 4: INSTANT MESSAGING IN AND OUT OF YOUR HOME NETWORK

This chapter looks at the increasingly popular communications method known as *instant messaging (IM)*. IM allows for real-time communication with other people. Email is a great solution when you have the time to wait for a response and it is a great leap over postal mail. Telephone conversations offer immediate responses. If you combine email with the immediacy of telephony you end up with instant messaging. IM is interactive, letting you communicate with one or more persons and exchange a good deal more information than can be done with email or the telephone over the same period. IM is not as demanding of your time and attention as a phone conversation; you can continue to work on other things and can even choose not to respond to a conversation that is ongoing for as long as you like. IM is more private; it gives you the ability to control whether anyone can see that you are available to receive instant messages, and you can decide who can and cannot send messages to you. You can send text with IM applications, and you can even use your audio and video hardware to communicate via voice and/or virtual face-to-face communications. These are among the reasons why IM has gained an incredible amount of popularity recently.

In this chapter you'll use Windows Messenger. This application is installed by default with all Windows XP installations, so it makes a natural choice as the IM platform in your home network. You can use Windows Messenger to communicate with one or many users on the Internet or on your local home network. If your computer is equipped with a sound card, a microphone, and speakers or a pair of headphones, you can use Windows Messenger to "talk" to another person on the network. Add a webcam, and you have full-fledged audio and video communications capabilities, which would allow someone working from a home office, for example, to attend audioconference and videoconference calls from the comfort of his or her own home.

To use the Windows Messenger application, you need a network connection and a .NET Passport account. The .NET Passport account is required whether you are communicating with people over the Internet or over your own local network because the list of contacts you see in Messenger is stored on a central server on the Internet. The advantage this offers is that your contacts are available to you regardless of where you are physically. So, for example, you could be away on a business trip with your laptop and still sign in to your Windows Messenger .NET Passport account and be able to communicate with people just as if you were on your home network. If you don't already have a .NET Passport account, don't worry; in this chapter you'll walk through the process of setting one up.

Getting Started with Windows Messenger

This section walks you through the steps required to get the Windows Messenger application configured for your home network. As described in this section, prior to using Windows Messenger, you need to perform a few steps to get it running properly. You need to sign in to your Passport account in order to use Windows Messenger. If you don't already have a Passport account, you need to create one. When you are not signed in, the icon looks as shown in Figure 5.1.

IM BACKGROUND

An early version of an IM program was first implemented on something called the PLATO system in the early part of the 1970s. The UNIX talk tool was the next IM system, and it was widely used in academic and research environments into the 1980s and 1990s as a way to communicate across the growing Internet. The UNIX talk tool was (and remains) a character-based method of IM, a far cry from today's graphic versions offering advertisements along with multimedia capabilities. Made available in 1996, ICQ was the first non-UNIX-based IM tool.

IM tools now include AIM, MSN, Yahoo, and Windows Messenger, to name a few. Each of these follows its own protocol, and while attempts have been made at creating a unified standard, they have for the most part failed. The landscape these days is very scattered unless you either happen to use the same IM as your friends or you have a multiprotocol IM client such as Trillian.

WINDOWS MESSENGER ON A VPN

When working from your home network, you may find that you need to connect to your company's network occasionally. Most corporate networks these days require a secure connection in the form of a virtual private network (VPN). If you make a VPN connection while you are in the middle of a Messenger session, your session may stop. Unfortunately, you will not see any indication of this other than the person on the other end of the conversation not responding to your messages. Although you might think that your conversation partner is just being obstinate, what is really going on is that when a VPN connection is made, the default gateway is changed from the default gateway that was in effect before the VPN connection was established to the gateway of the remote VPN. The bottom line in this type of situation is that your computer is reconfigured to use the default gateway on your remote corporate or ISP network. If you already have a connection to the Internet, independent of the VPN connection, there is really no reason to allow this to continue to happen. To fix the problem introduced by this situation, follow these steps:

1. Select Start, Control Panel and then select Network Connections.

2. Right-click your VPN connection and then click Properties.

3. On the Networking tab, select Internet Protocol (TCP/IP) and then click Properties.

4. On the Internet Protocol (TCP/IP) Properties page, click Advanced.

5. On the General tab, clear the Use Default Gateway on Remote Network check box.

Windows Messenger should then be started by default and will appear on the bottom left of the taskbar notification area of your screen.

To get Windows Messenger up and running, follow these steps:

1. Start Windows Messenger by either double-clicking its icon on the taskbar notification area or selecting Start, All Programs, Windows Messenger. The Add a .NET Passport to Your Windows XP User Account page appears (see Figure 5.2).

FIGURE 5.1

The Passport Wizard.

2. Click Next. The Do You Have an E-mail Address? page appears (see Figure 5.2).

3. Select the appropriate option and then click Next. If you chose Yes, Use My Existing E-mail Address, continue with step 4; if you chose No, Sign Me Up for a Free MSN Hotmail E-mail Address, skip to step 7.

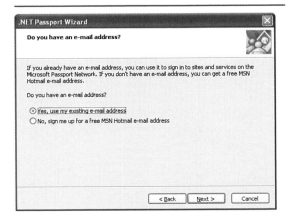

FIGURE 5.2

The Do You Have an E-mail Address? page.

FIGURE 5.3

The Have You Signed Up with the Microsoft Passport Network? page.

4. On the Have You Already Signed Up? page, if you have a Passport account, click Yes, Sign In with My Passport Network Credentials and then on the following page enter your Passport credentials to connect. Otherwise, click No, Sign Up Now and then click Next.

5. On the Sign Up with the Microsoft Passport Network page, click Next. You are taken to a web page where you create your passport account. When you have completed the process, you see the Have You Signed Up with the Microsoft Passport Network? page (see Figure 5.3).

6. Click Back and repeat step 4, this time signing in with your Passport credentials. Then go to step 9.

7. On the Sign Up with MSN Hotmail page, click Next. This takes you to a web page where you create your Hotmail account. When you have completed that process, you see the Have You Signed Up with MSN Hotmail? page (see Figure 5.4).

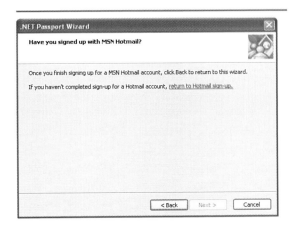

FIGURE 5.4

The Have You Signed Up with MSN Hotmail? page.

8. Click Back and repeat step 4, this time signing in with your MSN Hotmail credentials. Then go to step 9.

9. On the You're Done! page, click Finish (see Figure 5.5).

Depending on the version of Windows Messenger on your computer, you might be prompted to download a newer version. In this case, when Messenger starts, you see a screen like the one in Figure 5.6. If your computer has Windows XP with Service Pack 2, you probably have the latest version of Windows Messenger and don't need to worry about it. To download a newer version, click Yes and follow the prompts onscreen to complete the installation.

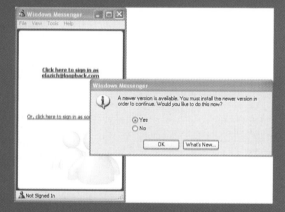

FIGURE 5.6

The Messenger version reminder.

Figure 5.6 shows a prompt that asks you to download a newer version of Windows Messenger before you can sign in. After you download a newer version, you are placed at the main screen, which looks as shown in Figure 5.7.

continues

FIGURE 5.5

Completing the Passport Wizard.

Setting Up Windows Messenger

The main Windows Messenger screen gives you an idea of the possible actions you can take. For example, you can add contacts with whom you can chat, send an instant message, send a file, or start a voice or video conversation. One of the things you will be doing with Messenger is communicating with people using IM, and before you can do so, you have to add to Messenger the contacts with whom you want to communicate.

To add contacts to Windows Messenger, follow these steps:

1. With Windows Messenger open, in the I Want To section, click Add a Contact. The How Do You Want to Add a Contact? page appears (see Figure 5.8).

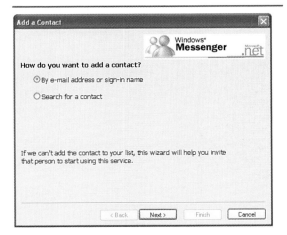

FIGURE 5.8

Adding a contact.

FIGURE 5.7

Windows Messenger.

2. Click By E-mail Address or Sign-in Name and then click Next.

3. On the next page, enter your contact's e-mail address and then click Next.

4. On the Success page (see Figure 5.9), click Next to add another contact or click Finish if you are done adding contacts.

You should now see your contact listed under All Contacts. The person you added to your contacts list gets a notification that you have added him or her to your contact list. That person has the option of allowing or denying you the ability to see when he or she is online. Your intended contact can also add you to his or her contact list at the same time (see Figure 5.10).

ABOUT PASSPORT

Microsoft provides Passport as a single sign-on solution. The idea is that you go to a central site (in this case, the Microsoft Passport site) and create an account that you will use on any website that supports Passport authentication. The nice thing about single sign-on is that you can move from site to site to site and not have to continually provide your credentials after the first site you connect to. (This, of course, assumes that each site in the sequence supports Passport authentication.) With Windows Messenger, Passport is used as the central authentication mechanism when you first sign on to your Messenger session.

FIGURE 5.9

Successfully adding a contact.

FIGURE 5.10

Add Contact notification.

To continue, your intended contact has to make a selection on the screen shown in Figure 5.10 and then click OK.

Having a Windows Messenger Conversation

You can now use Windows Messenger. The next step is to actually participate in an online conversation, using Windows Messenger. Keep in mind that as long as you have the email addresses of the people with whom you want to talk and they have allowed you to see when they are online, you can start a conversation with any of them, either on your local home network or somewhere out on the Internet at large. The following example features you and one of your children using IM. You are on the bedroom computer, and your child is supposed to be doing homework on the family room computer. Being a kid, your little angel tends to stray, and his attention drifts to online games and other frivolous activities, so you need to periodically check in to see how things are progressing. You could carry out this scenario by calling out to the child, but bedrooms tend to be a fair distance from family rooms, which means you'd have to raise your voice or go downstairs. Instead, you can take advantage of the technology offered by a tool such as IM to find out in real-time, without having to raise your voice, what is going on. Here's how you do it:

1. While signed in to Windows Messenger, double-click the contact (in this case, your son) with whom you want to start a conversation.

2. Type into the text box next to the Send button and then click Send. For the sake of this example, type **hello** and then click Send.

3. You and your recipient both receive a message window showing the conversation so far, like the one in Figure 5.11.

FIGURE 5.11

A Windows Messenger conversation.

Windows Messenger, like many other IM solutions, uses Session Initiation Protocol (SIP) to accomplish the communication capabilities you can achieve on your network. The details of SIP are beyond the scope of this book and may not be for the faint of heart. However, if you end up dealing with corporate scenarios as a user, you may encounter situations in which IM will not work because some administrators do not allow SIP to pass through their firewalls.

SIP is really intended to merge all communications so that in the near future you will make your telephone, video, IM, and any other communications sessions using SIP on an integrated platform. If you are dead set on learning more about SIP, you should start with where it was first defined as a proposed standard. As in many other cases, the Internet Engineering Task Force (IETF) proposed SIP. You can read all about it at www.ietf.org/rfc/rfc3261.txt.

Summary

You are quickly building up the capabilities of your home network. You have now created a wireless network, learned how to share files and printers, used your network as a jukebox, and learned how to use the Windows Messenger to communicate with others via IM in real time. This chapter is by no means an exhaustive resource on Windows Messenger or IM in general, and you are encouraged to read the online help for Windows XP. You can also find a wealth of information on IM by using the various Internet search engines, such as Google.

CHAPTER 6

Project 5: Creating and Sharing Video on Your Home Network

A WORD ABOUT DVD PLAYERS

The ability to create your own discs to play in a home DVD player is an exciting feature. However, when you're making your own discs, you need to keep in mind compatibility. Most modern DVD players offer the ability to play not only prerecorded DVDs but also those burned on the various DVD formats, including -R, +R, +RW, and various other combinations, depending on the manufacturer.

DVD -R was developed by Pioneer in 1997 and is the most compatible format available. The DVD +RW format offers the ability to write to the disc more than one time, which can be a great convenience. However, because the price of DVDs is so low, it can be a financial wash to simply buy more DVD -R discs than to buy the more expensive +RW version.

When purchasing blank DVDs, check the packaging to see what formats are supported, and if this information isn't printed on the box, you can most likely get the information from the retailer or by doing an online search for the product you are planning on buying to ensure that it will support the type of media you will use to create your own DVDs. If you want to author DVDs, and you want to be as compatible as possible with any DVD players you might purchase, then go ahead with DVD -R. It works, and it will continue to work for the foreseeable future. Prices seem to have become stable, and the format will not be obsolete tomorrow.

The downside is that at this time you cannot rely on rewritable formats to be compatible with any arbitrary player, old or new. This is getting better, as new players come to the marketplace and are more compatible with the rewritable formats. The DVD Forum has introduced a DVD-Multi logo to label players as compatible, including support for the DVD-RAM format.

Many homes have video cameras that are pulled out to capture the kids' first bike rides, trips to the beach, summer vacations, and various other activities. Many times, these videos end up being relegated to the closet and forgotten. You can customize movies of birthday parties by editing out all the dull parts and adding more excitement by creating titles or adding special effects. When you have a movie just the way you want it, you can share it with others and even create your own DVDs or video CDs that can be played in a DVD player or sent to relatives who can share in the experience. This chapter shows you how to get your precious memories into digital form and then share them or view them from any point in your home network.

Windows XP ships with an application called Windows Movie Maker that you can use for video capture, editing, and sharing. Unfortunately, Windows Movie Maker does not come with DVD or video CD authoring tools built in. However, if you have a DVD burner on your computer, you undoubtedly already have DVD authoring software and can refer to the manual that came with your product on how to create your own DVDs from the final videos that you create with Movie Maker.

Preparing to Get Your Videos to Your Computer

Before you can view your videos on your home network, you need to have some way of getting your videos from your tape collection into digital format. The consumer video market includes a large array of devices for videotaping special events. You may have VHS tapes, beta format tapes, 8mm videotapes, or miniDV tapes. The key to working with any of these media is putting the video in digital format and transferring it to your computer.

Video Capture

In digital video jargon, transferring video to your computer is called *video capture*. You can accomplish a capture by either connecting your equipment to a video capture card or by connecting to a FireWire port. The easiest way to tell which option is right for you is by looking at the owner's manual for your video camera. A section in the manual should deal with the various connectors available on your device. If your camera has audio input and output jacks, also known as RCA jacks, then your choice will have to be a video capture card. Fortunately, with Windows XP, setting up a video capture card is now far easier than it was in the past. However, you do have to open the case on your computer to install the card, and this alone can cause people to break into a cold sweat. But if you read the manual and follow the manufacturer's instructions, you should be up and running in no time. If the hardware installation proves too much for you to handle, you can certainly have the equipment installed at many of the larger computer retail outlets.

A WORD ABOUT DIGITAL CAMERAS

When you are considering digital video cameras, you'll find that there are a bewildering range of choices. In the end, you'll need to make a decision based on features and price. That means it's a good idea to understand the features of a camera so you can decide which ones are worth the extra money. Consumer camcorders come in five main formats:

▶ **MiniDV**—MiniDV gives you the highest quality because it stores your video directly in digital format; MiniDV is capable of producing professional-quality video. Digital tapes can be duplicated with very little loss of quality as compared to their analog counterparts. Most MiniDV camcorders on the market support IEEE 1394 (FireWire) connections, which lets you to transfer video and audio in digital format to your computer.

▶ **Standard 8 and Hi-8**—These formats offer video recording quality that is a step below what you find with MiniDV. Hi-8 camcorders have a better recording system than Standard 8 and use a high-quality metal tape, which results in a cleaner, sharper picture than Standard 8 format. Because the videotapes for both formats are compact, the camcorders are typically small, light, and very compact. This makes it easy for you to take this type of camera almost anywhere you might want to capture video.

▶ **VHS and S-VHS**—VHS and S-VHS provide good consumer-quality video recordings. The VHS cassette is larger than the 8mm formats, so the camcorder is larger and carries a bigger battery. Newer VHS

continues

camcorders use the compact VHS-C or S-VHS-C tapes, which contain the same tape in a compact format.

You should expect to find a FireWire port on virtually any digital camcorder. Depending on what you plan to do with your camcorder, you may need other ports as well. For example, you need A/V outputs to connect to a TV or a VCR.

Batteries are your key to using your camcorder, so you need to be sure that you have a spare in case your main battery fails. The length of battery life is very important, and you should plan on buying a battery rated for use that matches as closely as possible to the amount of time you plan on using the camcorder. You need to be careful about the time estimates on batteries, however, as they do not take into account things such as using your color viewfinder and zooming in and out. Each of these use more power than simply pointing your camera and capturing video, and you should keep this in mind when buying batteries.

By far the easier path for video capture is to use FireWire. With a FireWire port, your digital video camera becomes an extension of your computer system. Many computers come with FireWire ports as part of their standard package, and you can usually modify those that don't by installing a FireWire card in your computer. When you have FireWire, controlling your video camera with your software becomes very easy. This book assumes that you have a FireWire port on your computer and that your video camera supports a FireWire connection.

Capture Considerations

When you capture video from your camcorder, you are saving the video content to digital form, in a file that takes space on your local computer hard disk. A video capture can consume a large amount of disk space, so you need to consider the size of your hard disk for video captures of any great size. If you will be doing an appreciable amount of video capture, editing, and movie creation, you should consider a hard disk of 200GB or greater.

You also need to be aware of the format you choose for your capture. Two formats for video capture are supported by Movie Maker:

▶ **DV AVI**—DV AVI is the format most camcorders use when they capture video to tape. The DV AVI format is all you could ask for in terms of reliable reproduction of your videos. The resolution is at 720×480 pixels at 30 frames per second. The biggest disadvantage of the DV AVI format is that each minute of video takes 200MB of disk space. So with the one-hour tapes that are common in camcorders, you will fill your hard disk rather quickly unless you have a lot of space.

NOTE

Films shown at a movie theater are typically projected at 24 frames per second. There is a movement in the digital video industry to adopt the 24 frames per second as a standard, which is referred to as 24p. You may notice that your own videos don't have the same look and feel as you see in theaters. Part of the reason for this is that consumer video cameras capture video at roughly 30 frames per second. Some video editing software lets you add film grain to your video to achieve more of a film look. Windows Movie Maker offers an effect you can use in your videos to make it look more like film. In the end, though, don't be terribly disappointed if your videos don't have a film quality to them.

▶ **Windows Media Video (WMV)**—WMV, Microsoft's proprietary video format, offers great quality with the advantage of requiring a fraction of the amount of space of comparable DV AVI captures. As a matter of fact, some movie theaters are switching to digital projection techniques and are opting for the WMV format. The big drawback to the WMV format is that your video must be re-encoded before it can be stored in WMV format. Because camcorders store video in the DV AVI format, in order for the capture to wind up in the WMV format, the digital data must be converted by using a codec. (The term *codec* is shorthand for *coder–decoder*, referring to the functionality of this type of software, which is to code and decode streams of digital

WHAT IS FIREWIRE?

FireWire, developed primarily by Apple, was available in 1995. It is an IEEE standard referred to by the working group number 1394. So in the industry you hear people refer to FireWire as IEEE 1394. Products that support the IEEE 1394 standard have various names, depending on the manufacturer. Apple calls it FireWire, and because this is the most popular implementation, it has become synonymous with IEEE 1394. The terms i.link and Lynx are also used to refer to 1394. Whatever name is used, IEEE 1394 is a technology that is intended for applications that require a high data transfer rate. Video and multimedia take full advantage of the speeds offered by the FireWire solution.

FireWire can connect up to 63 devices, and it allows for peer-to-peer communications, meaning, for example, that a scanner can communicate with a printer without the computer's CPU being involved. Devices that support FireWire are typically things like external hard disks or digital video cameras. It is also possible to build a TCP/IP network over computers with a FireWire port for extremely fast data transfers. FireWire devices are typically connected to your computer by cables of various configurations. Figure 6.1 shows some of the cables you might encounter with FireWire devices.

FIGURE 6.1
FireWire cables.

continues

WHAT IS FIREWIRE? *continued*

With most things having to do with computer hardware and software, improvements are a fact of life. The original IEEE 1394 standard defined a mechanism for transferring data at a speed of 400Mbps (megabits per second). The successor to the original standard bumped up this ceiling to 800Mbps. Today, 1394a refers to the 400Mbps version, and 1394b refers to the 800Mbps version of FireWire.

data.) As a general rule, you lose video quality whenever you have to convert from one format to another.

You need to keep these formats and resolutions in mind when you reach the Video Setting page during a capture session with Windows Movie Maker. DV AVI offers the highest quality; if you accept the default setting, you will capture using WMV file formats, with a smaller picture size. If you want to use WMV, make sure to choose the High Quality setting under the Other Settings choice during the capture session. In general, if you will be viewing the finished video on your local computer screen, it may suffice to leave the capture at the default setting. If you are planning on sending the video back to your digital camcorder or want to view it on your DVD player, you will want the higher-quality resolution.

Getting Started with Windows Movie Maker

The Movie Maker application is installed by default with Windows XP. You access it by selecting Start, All Programs, Accessories, Window Movie Maker. This places you at the main screen of the Windows Movie Maker application, which will look as shown in Figure 6.2.

FIGURE 6.2

Windows Movie Maker.

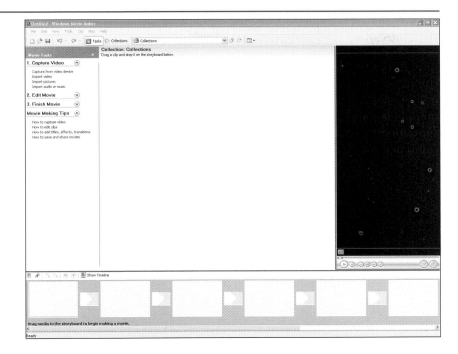

Capturing with Movie Maker

From the main screen of Windows Movie Maker, you have a number of options. There are three main tasks from which you can choose to start a session:

- **Capture Video**—You can use this task to capture video from your camcorder, import video from another source, and import still pictures and audio files.

- **Edit Movie**—You can use this task to add effects, add transitions, or make titles for your video projects.

- **Finish Movie**—You can use this task to save a completed video project to either your computer or to a CD, send it via email, place it on the Web for viewing, or send it back to your camcorder in its final edited form.

The first step in creating your video project is to get the video from your camcorder to your computer. To capture video with Windows Movie Maker, follow these steps:

1. In Windows Movie Maker, under Capture Video, select Capture from Video Device. The Captured Video File page appears (see Figure 6.3).

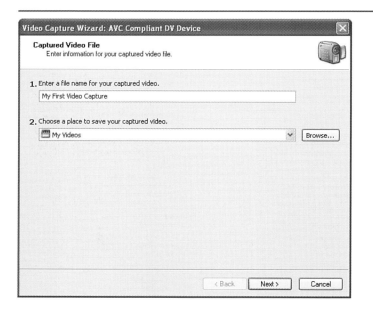

FIGURE 6.3

The Captured Video File page.

2. Enter a filename for your captured video, choose a place to save your video, and then click Next. The Video Setting page appears (see Figure 6.4).

NOTE

Recall our earlier discussion about the options available on the Video Setting page. Refer to the section "Capture Considerations," earlier in this chapter, for the choices available here.

3. Click Next. The Capture Method page appears (see Figure 6.5).

FIGURE 6.4

The Video Setting page.

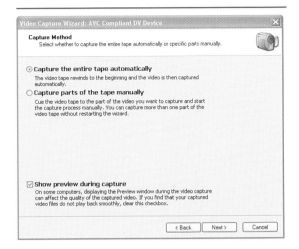

FIGURE 6.5

The Capture Method page.

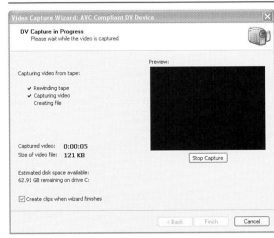

FIGURE 6.6

The DV Capture in Progress page.

NOTE

Note that on the Capture Method page you can capture either the entire tape or parts of the tape. It is easiest to capture the entire tape and then later edit out the parts you are not interested in—if you have the available disk space, of course. You also have the choice to see a preview of your tape during capture. You might want to turn off this feature if you have problems with erratic playback of your captured videos.

4. Click Next. You should now see the DV Capture in Progress page (see Figure 6.6).

You can stop the capture at any time by clicking the Stop Capture button on the DV Capture in Progress page.

Editing with Movie Maker

When your video capture is complete, the video clips that were created during the capture appear in the collection window, as shown in Figure 6.7.

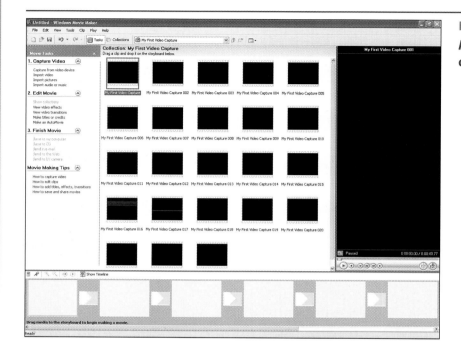

FIGURE 6.7

A video capture collection.

You edit your video project by following this step:

1. Drag the clips you want to include in your video to the storyboard. When you have a few clips included in your project, your screen should look something like the one shown in Figure 6.8. Notice that each clip appears in a separate box at the bottom of the screen, with a smaller shaded box between each clip.

NOTE

Clips are really nothing more than segments of video saved to a computer's hard disk. Windows Movie Maker can split your video into clips for you based on the scene breaks and timeline. This provides a convenient way for you to decide which pieces of video you want to include in your project.

FIGURE 6.8

Adding clips to the storyboard.

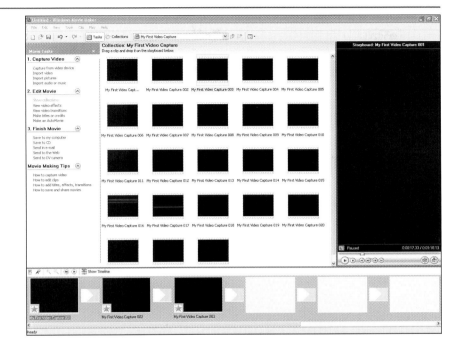

If desired, switch to Movie Maker's Timeline view, which shows your clips sequentially laid out.

> **NOTE**
>
> Movie Maker offers two ways to look at your developing video project. You can lay out your video in Storyboard view, where you see the graphic representation of the clip in a window next to each of the other clips that make up your project. Or you can opt for the Timeline view, which shows your video clips on a ruler representing elapsed time in the video project. Rather than viewing your clips in windows next to each other, the Timeline view lets you see how much time each clip and the entire project will take.

Adding Effects

You can use effects to add drama to your video. As a general rule, you should be conservative with effects: You don't want them to take over as the focus of the finished product. You can see the effects that Movie Maker offers by clicking the View Video Effects link under the Edit Movie section of the screen. To apply an effect, you click and then drag the desired effect to the clip on which you want to apply it. You can apply multiple effects to individual video clips, but before you do, put yourself in the place of the intended viewer to make sure that the effects do not end up detracting from the finished video. For example, it might make sense to have a single clip contain both the fade in and fade out effects for dramatic emphasis. You can also access effects by right-clicking a video clip in the storyboard or time-line and then clicking Video Effects. To see what an effect will look like, you can select the clip and then click Play in the player window on the right side of the screen. Figure 6.9 shows an example of the effects that are available with Movie Maker.

Adding Transitions

You can use transitions to create seamless connections between scenes in your video. For example, if you have video of a birthday party, you might want to ease the viewer between the opening of presents and the playing of party games. Transitions help you to control the mood and flow of a video. Like effects, transitions can be a veritable toy box for a person getting started with editing videos. You might feel like you have to use all these toys, but again, keep the viewer in mind and ask yourself if you really need the transitions you're considering. Using too many transitions can take away from the focus of the video.

You can see the available transitions under the Edit Movie section of the screen by clicking the View Video Transitions link. To apply a transition, click and then drag the desired transition between two clips either in the Storyboard view or the Timeline view. To see what a transition will look like, select the transition and then click Play in the player window on the right side of the screen.

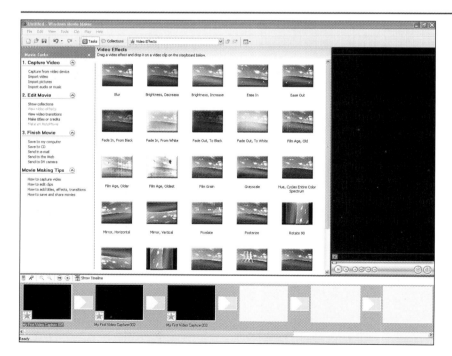

FIGURE 6.9

Movie Maker's video effects.

Adding Titles and Credits

You can use titles and credits to introduce the theme of your video and, where applicable, give credit to those who played a part in the making of the video. For example, if you were editing a video of a child's birthday party, you could use a title to indicate for whom the party was given. Titles can even be used in the midst of video to emphasize or reiterate a certain point.

You can see the available titles and credits under the Edit Movie section of the screen by clicking the Make Titles or Credits link. Unlike effects and transitions, titles and credits aren't listed as a menu of choices; rather, you select where you want text to appear in your video and you determine what the text should say. Figure 6.10 shows the choices.

You can control the title animation—that is, the way it moves, if at all, across the screen—and you can control the font and color of the text used for the title. You supply the text for the title (see Figure 6.10).

Movie Maker enables you to create credits that will appear at the end of the movie. You input the text for credits a little differently than you do for titles. Credits tend to be a list of people who either performed or were involved in the creation of the movie, so the text input screen appears as a two-column spreadsheet rather than as a free-form field (see Figure 6.11).

FIGURE 6.10

Title options.

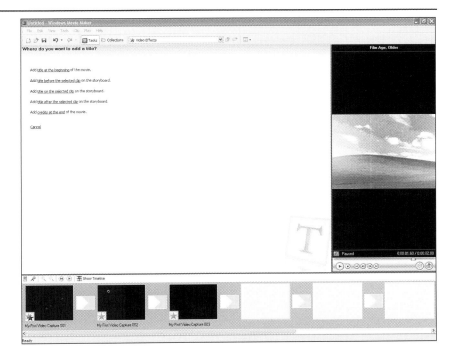

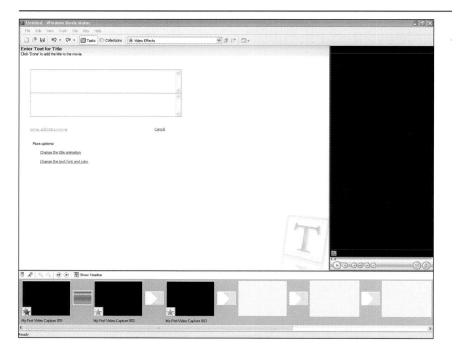

FIGURE 6.11
Title text.

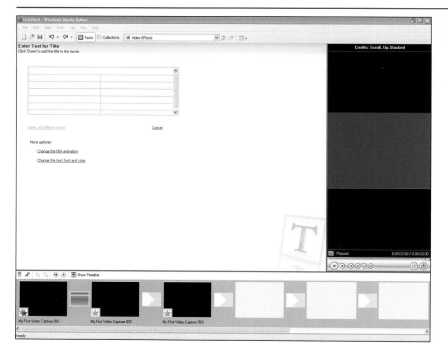

FIGURE 6.12
Entering credits.

Adding Finishing Touches to Your Movie

Now it's time to commit your movie to posterity, or at least to your hard disk. Movie Maker gives you a few options in this area. In this section, we concentrate on saving the movie to the local computer's hard disk and then sharing it with all the computers on your home network. However, after you save your movie, you can also send it as an email attachment, share it on the Web, save it to a CD, or even send it back in final form to your camcorder.

FIGURE 6.13
Saving your movie.

> **NOTE**
> Sending video clips via email is an option for only very short clips. Any lengthy video clips will be large files that don't work well as email attachments.

> **NOTE**
> Keep in mind that you can click the Show More Choices link on the Save Movie Wizard page to choose other settings for your saved movie file. Refer to the "Capture Considerations" section, earlier in this chapter, for more information.

To save a movie to your computer, follow these steps:

1. In Movie Maker, under Finish Movie, click Save to My Computer. The Saved Movie File page appears (see Figure 6.13).

2. Enter a filename for your movie and choose a folder in which to save your movie. Then click Next. The Movie Setting page appears.

3. Click Next. The Completing the Save Movie Wizard page appears.

4. Click Finish to complete the wizard.

Assuming that you accepted the default choices, your movie begins to play in Windows Media Player. From Chapter 3, "Project 2: Sharing Files, Printers, and Other Stuff on Your Network," you know how to share the folder where your videos are located. For other members of your home network to view your video work of art, they merely have to connect to the shared folder where you have placed the video file and double-click the file; Windows Media Player then begins to play the movie on that person's computer.

Summary

This chapter covers some of the basics of editing your own home videos. You have learned how to use Windows Movie Maker to capture video from your camcorder; edit that video by adding effects, transitions, and/or titles; and save a movie. Windows Movie Maker is a wonderful entry into the world of video editing. It does have limits, however, such as not allowing you to directly burn DVDs. But you can find many third-party applications to solve that problem. For example, Ulead Systems's Video Studio, Sonic's MyDVD, Pinnacle's Studio and Liquid Edition, Adobe Premiere, and a number of other applications offer varying feature sets to help you create great home movies.

CHAPTER 7

When Your Network Doesn't Work the Way It Should

At some point in the existence of your home network, problems are bound to arise. They can range from the mildly annoying yet simple to the excruciatingly aggravating and difficult. You can resolve most of them with a little logical thought about what is going on with your network.

In general, after you set up your network, it should just continue to work. However, when the unexpected happens, such as a thunderstorm knocking out your cable or DSL modem, you may have to perform some troubleshooting to get things back up and running. This chapter guides you through some of the most common problems you will encounter and how to resolve them.

Addressing TCP/IP Problems

Because TCP/IP is the communications protocol on which the very lifeblood of a home network depends, it stands to reason that if there is a problem at the TCP/IP level, you will not be able to get to anything outside your local computer. The symptoms you can expect to see when you experience problems with TCP/IP include an inability to use your web browser to connect to websites, an inability to connect to your shared video or audio library, and an inability to use shared files and printers.

The first thing to check in these cases is the physical connection between your computers. If your computers are networked using wires, you need to ensure that they are connected properly. If you are using wireless networking, you need to ensure that your wireless card is pushed in all the way and that your wireless access point is powered up. If the physical elements of your network are all in place and working correctly, you can use some of the invaluable tools that Windows provides for diagnosing and solving this problem. The following sections describe the Network Diagnostics tool and some of the available Windows command-line tools.

The Network Diagnostics Tool

The easiest method of troubleshooting network connectivity issues is by starting the Network Diagnostics tool, which is available in the Windows Help and Support Center. You can run this graphical tool to analyze various components of network connectivity and get a report that shows the results. To run the Network Diagnostics tool, follow these steps:

1. Select Start, Help and Support. The Help and Support Center appears.

2. Under Pick a Task, click Use Tools to View Your Computer Information and Diagnose Problems.

> **NOTE**
>
> You can also run the Network Diagnostics tool by selecting Start, Run and then typing netsh diag gui and clicking OK.

3. Under Tools, click Network Diagnostics, and then in the right side of the screen, click Scan Your System. A report like the one shown in Figure 7.1 appears.

4. Under Modems and Network Adapters in the Network Diagnostics tool report, click Network Adapters. The details of your network adapter appear. Look for the word FAILED (in red text) next to any item in this list. You can click to expand any item marked this way to get more information.

In the example shown in Figure 7.2, there is a problem with the default gateway. This example is from my home network and is a good example of needing some understanding of the network in order to interpret results. On my network, the 10.0.0.1 address is a firewall computer that is acting as my gateway to the Internet as well. I have intentionally turned off the ability to process ICMP packets on my firewall as a security measure. So in the case of this network, this is not really a problem, as long as we understand what is happening.

Command-Line Tools

Those of us who have been around networking long enough remember running applications and utilities from a somewhat archaic command interpreter. In DOS it was the famous **C:>** prompt, and in UNIX it was the shell prompt, which would vary, depending on the shell of your choice (for example, the C shell, Bourne shell, or Korn shell). Under both UNIX and DOS, interaction with the computer was basically the same: You typed a command and pressed Enter, and the computer displayed the results in text and/or numeric form. There were no windows or pretty pictures and icons; you simply got a response to the command that you gave to the interpreter. In those days, the **ping** utility was extremely useful as a network troubleshooting tool. **ping** is still available and is still just as useful as ever.

You use the **ping** utility to send Internet Control Message Protocol (ICMP) packets to the intended destination. If the destination replies, you know that the connection between the two computers is working. You use the **ping** utility at a command prompt, which you can access on a Windows system by selecting Start, All Programs, Accessories. Figure 7.3 shows an example of using the **ping** utility.

The Network Diagnostics tool gathers information about your computers to help you solve network problems. It also lets you run a variety of tests to gather information to help you solve problems with your network. The program scans your computer to see if you have network connectivity and whether the programs required for proper network functions are running on your computer. The output of the tool is a graphic representation of information to help you quickly identify what might be wrong with the networking components of your network. All scans are performed only on your local computer to maintain privacy and the security of your data.

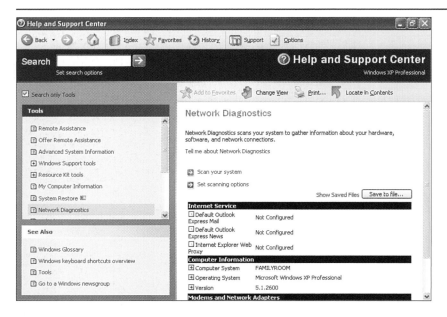

FIGURE 7.1

The Network Diagnostics tool.

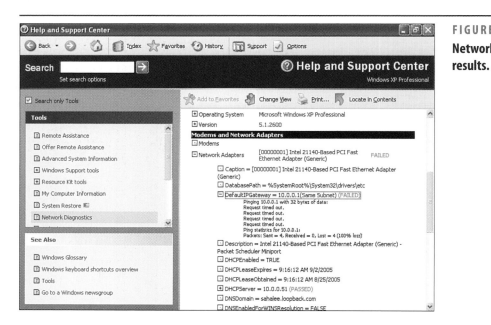

FIGURE 7.2

Network Diagnostics tool results.

FIGURE 7.3
The ping utility.

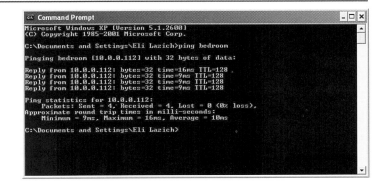

FIGURE 7.3
The ping utility.

If you see replies to your **ping**, you know that the two computers can communicate just fine, and you can move on and focus your troubleshooting efforts elsewhere.

However, if all the replies show up as "Request timed out," then either your computer or the destination computer has a TCP/IP problem. To narrow down where the problem is, you should check network connectivity, moving from your local computer outward, until you either encounter success or find a point where you are not able to communicate any further. This is sort of analogous to the "get your own house in order first" school of thought. In general, you should follow these steps and stop wherever you run into a problem: While this approach may not work for more complex environments, for a home network, it should get you up and running. Firewalls and packet-filtering routers and switches complicate this simplistic approach to troubleshooting.

1. **ping** your own computer first, using one of the following commands:

   ping 127.0.0.1

   ping localhost

NOTE

Each computer on a TCP/IP network maintains what is called the *local loopback address*. This address is expressed as 127.0.0.1 and is also known by the name localhost and can be used as a way to test whether TCP/IP is loaded and working properly on your local computer. If a ping to localhost or 127.0.0.1 fails, there is a problem with the TCP/IP drivers loaded on your machine, and you probably need to reinstall them. This is not as catastrophic as it might seem. You can do it by selecting Start, Run and then typing netsh int ip reset resetlog.txt and clicking OK.

2. **ping** your computer's IP address.

TIP

You can find the IP address for the computers in your network by typing ipconfig /all in a command prompt window. Figure 7.4 shows an example of the output from ipconfig. Among the items you'll see are the computer's IP address, the default gateway IP address, and DNS and WINS server information. If your computer shows an IP address in the form 169.254.x.y, your computer is using Automatic Private IP Addressing (APIPA). This means that your computer attempted to use Dynamic Host Configuration Protocol (DHCP) to obtain an IP address but was   unable to do so because it was unable to contact a DHCP server. See the section "Fixing IP Address Problems," later in this chapter, for more information.

3. **ping** the IP address of another computer on your network. If you receive no response from the other computer but have been successful to this point, the problem is likely with the remote computer.

NOTE

Try to ping multiple computers before you conclude that the problem is with remote computers.

4. **ping** the address of your default gateway. This may or may not be useful. In general, if your gateway responds to **ping** requests, you can check along the communications path to ensure that data is reaching its destination. Nowadays, however, these types of devices often do not respond to **ping** requests as a security measure.

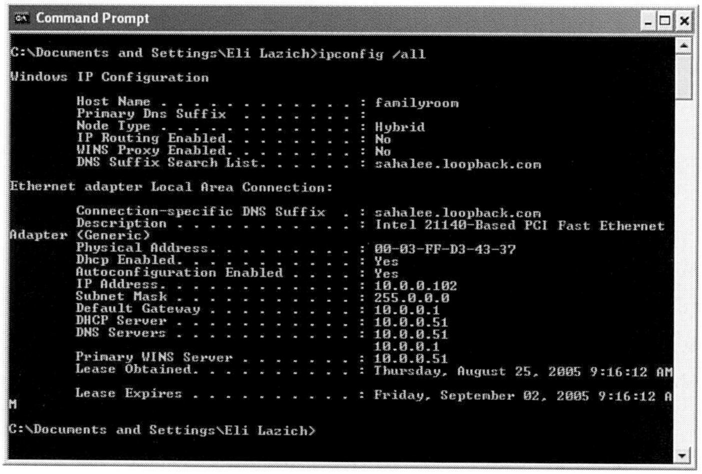

```
Command Prompt                                          _ □ x

C:\Documents and Settings\Eli Lazich>ipconfig /all

Windows IP Configuration

        Host Name . . . . . . . . . . . . : familyroom
        Primary Dns Suffix  . . . . . . . :
        Node Type . . . . . . . . . . . . : Hybrid
        IP Routing Enabled. . . . . . . . : No
        WINS Proxy Enabled. . . . . . . . : No
        DNS Suffix Search List. . . . . . : sahalee.loopback.com

Ethernet adapter Local Area Connection:

        Connection-specific DNS Suffix  . : sahalee.loopback.com
        Description . . . . . . . . . . . : Intel 21140-Based PCI Fast Ethernet
Adapter (Generic)
        Physical Address. . . . . . . . . : 00-03-FF-D3-43-37
        Dhcp Enabled. . . . . . . . . . . : Yes
        Autoconfiguration Enabled . . . . : Yes
        IP Address. . . . . . . . . . . . : 10.0.0.102
        Subnet Mask . . . . . . . . . . . : 255.0.0.0
        Default Gateway . . . . . . . . . : 10.0.0.1
        DHCP Server . . . . . . . . . . . : 10.0.0.51
        DNS Servers . . . . . . . . . . . : 10.0.0.51
                                            10.0.0.1
        Primary WINS Server . . . . . . . : 10.0.0.51
        Lease Obtained. . . . . . . . . . : Thursday, August 25, 2005 9:16:12 AM

        Lease Expires . . . . . . . . . . : Friday, September 02, 2005 9:16:12 A
M

C:\Documents and Settings\Eli Lazich>
```

FIGURE 7.4

ipconfig output.

5. **ping** a well-known site on the Internet, such as www.google.com or www.microsoft.com. Try several sites before concluding that there is a problem in this step.

> **NOTE**
>
> Recall from earlier in this chapter that my default gateway would not respond to ping packets when I used the Network Diagnostics tool. Many sites on the Internet employ the same policy, as a security measure, and you may not get any response whatsoever when attempting to ping them. This is why you should try multiple destinations before coming to a conclusion.

If you don't find a problem until step 5, your problem is not a TCP/IP problem, and you should next look for domain name system (DNS) problems, as described later in this chapter, in the section "Diagnosing and Fixing DNS Problems."

Fixing IP Address Problems

DHCP is used on most networks these days because it provides ease of connectivity for both users and the network administrator. Users can freely move with their desktops and/or notebook computers to any network owned by the organization. The alternative is to have every computer user understand the details of static IP addressing as it relates to the network on

which they connect, and that is often more information than the average network user needs, not to mention a source of extra headaches for the network administrator.

Problems with DHCP can make it appear as if the network is the problem. DHCP provides a method by which clients on a TCP/IP network can dynamically obtain IP addresses. The way this is implemented in practical terms is that a server is configured to provide IP addresses to a specific range of clients. When a client's operating system starts, part of the startup process sends a broadcast message searching for a response from a DHCP server. If a DHCP server responds, it sends an IP address offer to the client, which ends up going to the client's IP address. When this process doesn't work, the computers are unable to obtain IP addresses and appear with APIPA addresses. To troubleshoot these types of problems, you need to take a look at the details of your TCP/IP configuration, which you can do by following these steps:

1. Select Start, Control Panel. The Control Panel appears.

2. Double-click Network Connections or, if you are using Category view, click Network and Internet Connections and then click Network Connections. A list of your network connections appears.

3. Double-click the network connection that you want to explore and then on the connection status window that appears, click the Support tab (see Figure 7.5).

FIGURE 7.5
Local area connection status.

4. Click Details for more information and then click Repair to attempt automatic recovery of your TCP/IP configuration.

5. If clicking Repair does not fix your problem, click the General tab of the connection status window and then examine the Activity section, which shows the amount of traffic being sent or received by your computer. If you watch this screen for a short time and see that your computer is sending but not receiving traffic, you can be reasonably certain that there is either an addressing or network problem.

Diagnosing and Fixing DNS Problems

DNS is used on TCP/IP-connected networks to convert computer names to IP addresses. For example, you can type in **www.microsoft.com**, and DNS converts that to an IP address. DNS exists because it is much easier for humans to remember a name than a cryptic number. However, DNS creates a layer of abstraction over the information that is required for connections to successfully complete. Any time you take a step away from a very simple system, there is the opportunity for error, and DNS is no exception. The following are two of the things to check when trying to diagnose potential DNS issues:

▸ **Check to make sure you have the correct DNS Servers configured in your TCP/IP settings**—You should check the detailed settings for your TCP/IP configuration to ensure that you have the DNS servers that are recommended by your ISP.

▸ **Check with your ISP to make sure it is not having problems**—It is worth taking the time to call your ISP's tech support line to find out whether the ISP is experiencing any problems that might be affecting your network. Many ISPs have web pages you can visit to check on current network status, and doing this can save you time and effort when troubleshooting.

▸ **Check your VPN settings**—If you connect to a VPN at your office, you may lose the ability to connect to the Internet. As discussed in Chapter 5, "Project 4: Instant Messaging in and out of Your Home Network," in the sidebar "Windows Messenger on a VPN," what ends up

THE BROWSER SERVICE

happening is that when you make a VPN connection, your computer has routing reconfigured to send all traffic through your corporate network, which may or may not offer the ability to send your request back to the Internet. You can follow the steps outlined in the sidebar in Chapter 5 to resolve this issue.

▶ **Clear your DNS cache**—You can resolve any temporary DNS problems by running **ipconfig /flushdns** from a command prompt. This has the effect of clearing your DNS cache and forcing your computer to obtain name resolution all over.

Fixing Problems Connecting to Other Computers on Your Network

One really annoying situation is looking for shared resources on other computers in your home network and not seeing any other computers available, let alone the resources you are trying to access. Windows networks use the browser service to maintain a list of the available computers and a list of what is shared on each computer when you operate in a workgroup environment such as the home network. Typically, this is a time-sensitive action, and if you wait just a few minutes, the list updates, and you can see your destination. You can also connect by using the path to the

The browser service is a rather complicated service that causes a list of available networked computers to appear on your screen. In general, you should not have to wait any longer than 24 minutes for resources to appear, and in small networks you should most likely not wait more than 12 minutes. If you end up waiting longer, something serious may be going on. For a detailed discussion of the browser service, see Microsoft Knowledge Base article 188001, which is available at http://support.microsoft.com/default.aspx?scid=kb;en-us;188001.

computer, such as **computername**\
sharename, to circumvent the browser service
and the potential delay imposed by the collection of available resources. In addition, you
can try executing **net view \\computername**
from a command prompt.

Optimizing Network Performance

Network performance is a tricky thing to quan-
tify because it's subjective. In some cases,
people complain about the response time of
the network when the traffic is at levels that
are actually considered acceptable response
times. Perception is often based on a user's
view of reality at the moment. If you have an
important presentation due in an hour, the
network is liable to seem slower to you than it
is if you have two weeks to finish your
presentation.

There are ways to objectively measure the
performance of your network and make
changes accordingly. The Windows Task
Manager shows performance numbers for your
system overall and for your network in particular. To reach the Task Manager, you can either
right-click an empty area of the taskbar and
then click Task Manager or you can press
Ctrl+Shift+Esc. Figure 7.6 shows an example of
the Task Manager.

FIGURE 7.6
The Task Manager.

You can select the Task Manager's Performance
and Networking tabs to see the load on your
computer:

▶ **Performance tab**—On the Performance
tab, you can get an idea of how busy your
computer is by looking at the CPU Usage
section of the screen. If this number stays
at or around 100% consistently, you
should look for a process that is taking
more than its share of CPU time. To find a
process that is using excessive CPU time,
you select the Processes tab and then click
the CPU column to sort. You then look for
a process that is consistently using a large
amount of CPU time, somewhere around
50% or more, on a continuous basis. When
you identify such a process, you can stop it

by right-clicking the process name and then clicking End Process. You just need to be sure not to try to stop the System Idle Process, which indicates how much time the CPU is idle.

▶ **Networking tab**—The Networking tab shows the utilization for each of the network cards installed in your computer. On a typical home network, you don't see enough activity to overly tax your NICs. You should check this screen if your network feels slower than usual. I recommend that whenever you deal with a network, you should set a baseline. The baseline in this case would be a check of network utilization during normal computer use that you can later compare to usage that seems unacceptable.

Fixing Unresponsive Applications

From time to time, for reasons well beyond the scope of this book, applications hang and become unresponsive, no matter what you try to do. In these cases, you might have to resort to terminating the application forcefully, as described shortly.

Before you terminate an application forcefully, however, you need to eliminate the obvious; that is you should be aware of the flow of the application and what it might be expecting to happen next. For example, if you are in the middle of a setup program for a new application you are installing and you switch to another screen, the setup program will eventually reach a point where it is expecting input

from you to complete what it needs to do. You can switch among the active applications by pressing Alt+Tab. When you reach the window that is expecting input, you may be able to provide what is needed and simply move on.

In other cases, you may have to forcefully terminate an application. To do this, you have to follow these steps:

1. Start the Task Manager by either right-clicking an empty area of the taskbar and then clicking Task Manager or by pressing Ctrl+Shift+Esc.

2. In the Task Manager, select the Applications tab.

3. To force an application that is not responding to close, click the End Task button in the Task Manager. A window appears, asking you to confirm your selection.

4. Click OK, and your unresponsive application closes.

Summary

This chapter covers quite a bit of ground related to troubleshooting problems you may encounter on your home network. It's important to keep in mind that you really cannot expect to effectively deal with problems unless you have an idea of how things work when all is well. In my experience, when you understand the intended path of a process, you are better equipped to fix a broken component of that process.

It is easy to get caught up in the apparent vastness of something like networking. If you take it a step at a time, though, and break the seemingly larger problem down into more manageable chunks, you can solve as you go along. This chapter describes some of the tools you can use in your troubleshooting efforts. This is by no means an exhaustive list, but it should be enough to get you started. If your interests take you beyond what is covered here, you can use your favorite search engine to find quite a bit of additional useful troubleshooting information.

CHAPTER 8

Bonus Project: Creating Your Own Website

Even though you have just about reached the end of this book, you have only begun your adventure in home networking. This last chapter walks you through how to create your own website. With the information in this chapter, you can create a family website where everyone can go for common information, relatives can visit for the latest family photos, and you can even have your own weblog (blog).

In order to create a website, you need two key components: a web server and some way to create web pages. That is exactly what you will learn about in this chapter.

Running Your Own Web Server

With the Windows XP operating system, you do not have a web server installed by default. You have to install the web server Internet Information Server (IIS) yourself. IIS isn't automatically installed with Windows XP because workstations do not typically serve content via the Web. Security concerns also drive the decision to not install a web server by default. With a web server installed, the so-called attack footprint is larger. This essentially means that hackers have more of an area on your computer to try to break into. Web server security flaws have been the source of some notorious security breaches, and the exclusion of this software from desktop systems limits the vulnerability.

Understanding the World Wide Web

The World Wide Web was invented as a way for scientists to exchange research information. Tim Berners-Lee invented the World Wide Web in 1989 as a way to exchange hypertext media on a global scale. While working at the CERN particle physics laboratory, Berners-Lee wrote the first web browser and server in 1990, and the world has been drastically altered since. In the early days of the Web, e-commerce was unheard of, and the Web was mostly used for research. I recall asking a manager to invest in an Internet connection back in the early 1990s and being told that the Internet was a neat toy, but it wouldn't amount to anything commercial. Looking back now, we can see how far this technology has come in a relatively short time.

The Web is a simple enough concept: A client requests something from a server, and the server responds with the data requested. The data in question is essentially a document with tags that identify how the text should appear on the page. These tags are part of Hypertext Markup Language (HTML), and the protocol that is used to transfer documents between clients and servers is called Hypertext Transfer Protocol (HTTP). You should keep in mind that HTTP by itself can accomplish nothing; it relies on TCP/IP to route data to the appropriate computers. You should also keep in mind that TCP/IP is unable to perform its task without the underlying physical connection of your wired or wireless network cards, switches, and/or hubs. Everything in the Web is connected, and the entire network infrastructure is made up of individual components that rely on the functionality provided by other components in order for the whole thing to work.

Installing IIS

As mentioned previously, before you can host a web server, you need to have a web server installed. Because you're running Windows XP, IIS is the most logical server choice because it is provided with the operating system.

> **NOTE**
>
> You can use other web servers rather than IIS. The Apache server is probably the most popular alternative, and it is available free of charge from www.apache.org. The reasons for installing other web servers have to do with application and feature compatibility and support. If you end up getting into any serious web development, these issues may become a concern, but for your home network, IIS should be adequate. You should just be aware that there are alternatives available.

To install IIS, follow these steps:

1. Select Start, Control Panel. The Control Panel appears.

2. Click Add or Remove Programs. The Add or Remove Programs window appears (see Figure 8.1).

3. Click Add/Remove Windows Components in the left side of the window. The Windows Components Wizard appears.

4. Scroll down to and the click the check box next to Internet Information Services (IIS), as shown in Figure 8.2, and then click Next. The Completing the Windows Components Wizard page appears.

> **NOTE**
>
> You need access to either your Windows XP CD or a location on your hard disk where you have copied the contents of that CD. You are prompted at this point to provide the CD (or point to the correct hard drive location) if you don't already have the CD in your computer. When you have checked the box for IIS, you should click the Details button to see what else is being installed on your computer. For example, the SMTP service will be selected for installation, and for the purposes of a home network where you will simply be serving web pages, this is unnecessary. You can clear the check box next to SMTP to eliminate the installation of this component and reduce the security exposure that would have otherwise resulted. Because this project will be created using Microsoft FrontPage, you need to install the FrontPage Server extensions by clicking the check box next to that option.

5. Click Finish.

6. Close Add or Remove Programs and then close Control Panel.

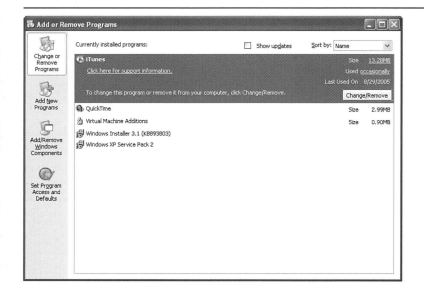

FIGURE 8.1

The Add or Remove Programs window.

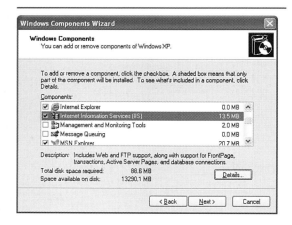

FIGURE 8.2
The Windows Components Wizard.

Exploring IIS

Now that you have IIS installed, it's time to see what you have. Open Internet Explorer, either from the Start menu or by double-clicking its desktop icon. To see the contents of your local web server, type **http://localhost** into the Address field of Internet Explorer and then press Enter. The content that your web server offers up comes from the **c:\inetpub\wwwroot** folder of the local hard disk of your computer. So any time you want to make a web page available, you need to place the file in that location. After you load the web page, the screen shown in Figure 8.3 should appear.

FIGURE 8.3

The default IIS web page.

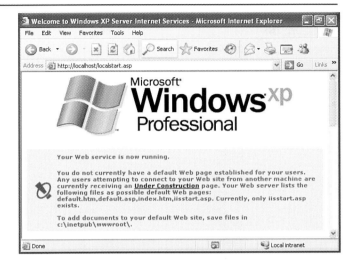

You should notice that you now have two web browser windows open: one that confirms that your web server is now installed and running and another that shows the IIS online help system. You can use the online help system to learn more about IIS. The other page that's now open lets you know that anyone accessing the page on your web server across the network will receive a page notifying them that your site is under construction. To see what it looks like from another machine, enter **http://***computername* in the Address field of the web browser on another computer on your network. You should see a page similar to the one in Figure 8.4.

Looking at IIS Configuration

Now that you have installed and begun to explore IIS, you are almost ready to create your own website. But first, you need to take a brief look at managing your web server. Follow these steps to start the IIS management console:

1. Select Start, Control Panel to open the Control Panel.

2. If you're in Category view, select Performance and Maintenance and then Administrative Tools. If you're in Classic view, click Administrative Tools. The Administrative Tools page appears.

3. Double-click Internet Information Services. The Internet Information Services page appears.

A NOTE ABOUT SECURITY

If your copy of Windows XP has been updated to include Service Pack 2, you will likely not be able to access your web server. This is because Service Pack 2 includes the Windows Firewall, which blocks such traffic. You therefore need to configure your web server to allow communications on TCP port 80, which is the default communications port for HTTP. To configure Windows Firewall in this way, follow these steps:

1. Open the Control Panel by selecting Start, Control Panel and then click Security Center. The Windows Security Center appears.

2. Under Manage Security Settings For, click Windows Firewall. The Windows Firewall page appears.

3. Select the Advanced tab and then click Settings under Network Connection Settings. The Advanced Settings page appears.

4. Click the check box next to Web Server (HTTP) and then click OK twice.

5. Close the Security Center and then close the Control Panel.

This procedure opens port 80 so that your web server can receive requests for web pages and respond accordingly.

4. Expand your computer and then expand the Web Sites folder by clicking on the plus sign next to each.

5. Right-click Default Web Site and then click Properties. The Default Web Site Properties page appears.

6. Select the Documents tab. The Documents tab shows what documents are served by default if a browser does not specify a particular document in the Address field. The order in which these documents are listed is their priority order. If you have both a **default.htm** and a **default.asp** file in the directory, **default.htm** is returned first.

The rest of the tabs in the IIS Manager control various aspects of the web server's operation and/or security settings. While they are very important, these topics are beyond the scope of this book. You can read the online help to get a better understanding of these and other aspects of IIS.

FIGURE 8.4

The Under Construction web page.

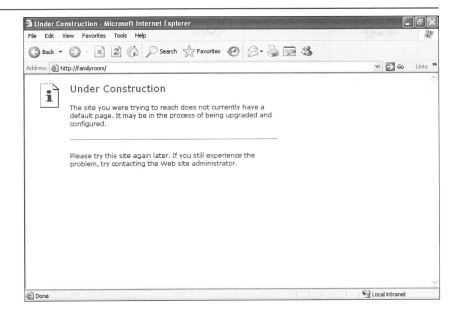

Creating Your Own Website

Before you can create your own website, you need some way to edit the files that will be served by your web server. This could be as simple and rudimentary as using the Notepad editor that comes with Windows, or it could be as complex as using a full-fledged web development environment, with all kinds of bells and whistles.

You need to keep in mind a few requirements when creating web pages. Recall that earlier we talked about HTML as the language used to create web pages. HTML defines each page as containing text between a pair of tags. *Tags* can be thought of as notes to the web server and the browser, letting them know what to do with the text within these tags. A tag pair consists of a beginning tag defined by the bracket pair <> and an ending tag defined by the bracket pair </>. Each HTML document must have at the very least the <html> and <body> tag pairs, along with their associated ending tag pairs, </html> and </body>. You also typically see the <title></title> tag pairs, which define the title of the page that is displayed on web browsers.

While you can certainly install everything you need on the computers of your home network to run a website, there are free or fee-based alternatives. Many sites offer you the ability to create a website for little or no cost. The advantage to you is that your computers are not burdened with the additional overhead of running a web server. The maintenance of the website becomes the responsibility of the company providing web hosting services. You can find these services in a variety of places on the Internet by searching for free websites. One particular site that is free and appears to offer quite a bit is www.freewebs.com.

Free and pay sites alike involve certain restrictions that you can avoid by running your own web server. For example, you will invariably find a restriction on the amount of space you can use on a hosted website. Some of the things offered at the freely available web hosting sites are photo albums, blogging tools, e-commerce capability, and many more features you might want included in your site. You need to sign up for an account before you begin creating your free website. Using one of these sites can be a great way to ease into running your own website with minimal effort. As an example of how easy it is to create your own site with the free hosting solutions, my nine-year-old son has created a site with friends of his, and between them, they have no knowledge of what a web server is, let alone how to run one.

Creating a Web Page by Using Notepad

To see for yourself how easy it is to create a basic web page by using Notepad, follow these steps:

1. Select Start, Run, type **notepad**, and then click OK. The Notepad editor appears.

2. Type the following in Notepad:

   <html>

   <title>My First Web Page</title>

   <body>

   This is my first web page

   </body>

   </html>

3. Select File, Save As. The Save As dialog box appears.

4. Ensure that the Save as Type field is set to All Files, type **myhtmlpage.html** for the filename, select **c:\inetpub\wwwroot** as the location to save the files, and then click Save.

5. To view the page you just made, open Windows Explorer, navigate to the My Documents folder, and double-click the file **myhtmlpage.html**. Internet Explorer starts, showing you the contents of the page you just created, without the tags you typed in. (Remember that the tags are used as markup to define how the contents of the page are to be displayed.)

NOTE

Another way to view the page you just created is to enter http://localhost/myhtmlpage.html in the address field of your web browser.

Creating a Web Page by Using FrontPage

You have seen how you can use a simple application such as Notepad to create web pages. However, many full-featured web page editors are available, including Macromedia's Dreamweaver, Adobe's Go Live, and a number of shareware or freeware utilities you can find by searching the Web. Different editors give you varying degrees of functionality, but in my opinion what you want for a home network if you don't really care to become an expert on web page development is what is commonly referred to as a WYSIWYG (what you see is what you get) editor. With this type of editor, the page you develop looks exactly like the page that will be seen in a web browser, so you can get a feel for the user experience. (Remember that when you use Notepad to create a web page, you type tags and don't really know what the page looks like until you load it in a web browser for the first time.)

Because you have the Windows XP operating system and you likely already have at least some of the Office applications, in this section you'll use FrontPage to develop a web page. FrontPage is a WYSIWYG editor and is available as a trial edition so that you can try it before you decide to purchase. The other nice benefit to using FrontPage is that it provides a wealth of templates from which you can create your own websites.

Entire books have been written about HTML. It is an extensive language that defines not only the tags that are required for a barebones page (such as the one used in this example) but also more complicated, interactive web pages as well. You could spend many hours reading about HTML and all its various nuances and still only scratch the surface of what you can do with it.

The World Wide Web Consortium (W3C) is a good starting point for learning more about HTML. You can visit www.w3c.org for more information. Figure 8.5 shows an example of what you'll find on the W3C website. Look under the section heading W3C A to Z and then click the HTML link, which takes you to various documents describing the language. You can find interesting articles, language specifications, and even tutorials here.

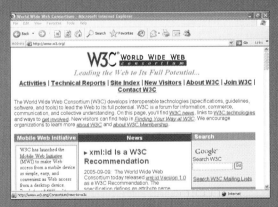

FIGURE 8.5
The W3C website.

Aside from FrontPage, you have many options when it comes to creating web pages. Adobe offers a product called GoLive, among many other content-creation tools. Macromedia offers a product called Dreamweaver, in addition to other content-creation tools. With these and the other components offered by these companies, you can create a very compelling website. If your web page designs need to go beyond the basics of getting some text and maybe a bit of graphics onscreen, you might want to take a look at these products. You can get very advanced with each of them, as well as with some of the freeware and shareware web editors available. For example, you could integrate dynamic elements in your web pages by using something like Macromedia's Flash in addition to the content you develop with the Web editor itself. This is done on many sites, for example, to achieve animation in the form of online games. When you get started in this area, your interests and the interests of the audience you are targeting with your web pages determine the toolset you end up using.

You could also use Microsoft Word to create web pages. A number of useful templates are available on the Microsoft Office website for Word as well as for FrontPage. FrontPage offers a number of features not available with Word, but if your needs are as simple as typing content into a document and then posting it on the Web, you might want to consider Word as your solution.

You can get the trial version of FrontPage from www.microsoft.com/frontpage. After you install FrontPage, you can open it by selecting Start, All Programs, Microsoft Office, Microsoft Office FrontPage 2003. The interface you see should look like the one shown in Figure 8.6.

Among the features built into FrontPage is the ability to create web pages from templates. Templates allow you to easily create pages based on pre-created standard forms. You can customize a template to meet your specific needs. To create a web page by using a template, follow these steps:

1. In FrontPage, select File, New. The New dialog box appears.

2. Under New Web Site, click One Page Web Site. The Web Site Templates page appears.

3. On the General tab, click Personal Web Site. Then, under Options, click the drop-down list and enter **C:\inetpub\wwwroot** as the location, and then click OK (see Figure 8.7).

FIGURE 8.6
Microsoft FrontPage.

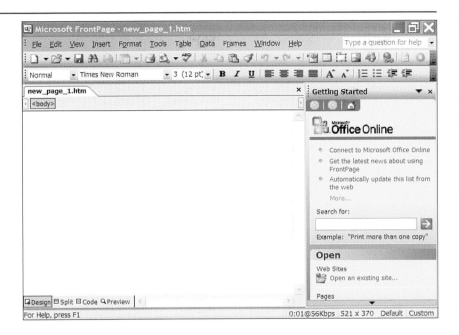

FIGURE 8.7
Website templates.

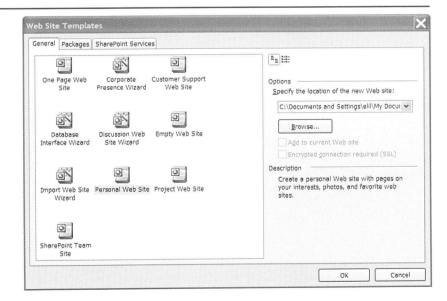

You are now taken to the main navigation window of FrontPage, which looks as shown in Figure 8.8. From this window you can move between the pages that make up a website and see the relationships among those pages. For example, **index.htm** is a standard file that is used as a default page for websites. This would be an appropriate place to provide any introductory or high-level information you want any visitor to your site to have.

4. To edit the main page for your site, double-click index.htm. A WYSIWYG display of the main page appears. You see the page as it looks to viewers on the right side of the window (see Figure 8.9).

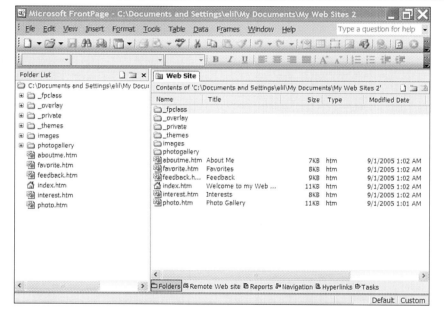

FIGURE 8.8

Navigating your website.

FIGURE 8.9
Editing your website.

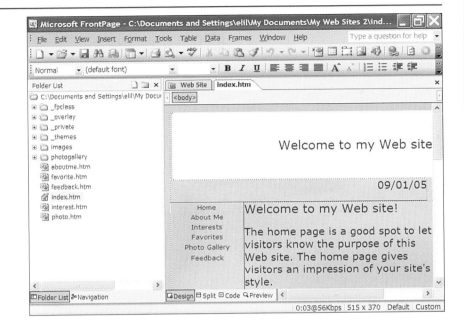

5. Replace the placeholder text from the template with your choice of content. When you are finished with the page, make sure to save it by selecting File, Save.

NOTE

FrontPage offers a handy feature called *publishing* that lets you publish the content you have edited on your local computer to a remote web server. While this topic is beyond the scope of this book, you might want to take a look at FrontPage's online help to get an idea of what you can do with this feature.

Summary

In this chapter you learned a little of the history of the World Wide Web. You installed your own web server and configured the optional components to suit the home networking environment. You then began the process of creating and publishing your very own website. From here, you can edit your content to suit the needs of your application. With a little more exploration of the capabilities in FrontPage, you can create imaginative and interactive websites. Visitors to your site could learn anything you wanted to share with them.

At this point, you have taken a little fledgling network from the conceptual stages and built it into something that can provide productivity and entertainment. I hope you've had fun learning how to get your computers communicating with each other. Along the way, you have hopefully picked up a bit more knowledge about technology than you thought you might. The topics in this book are by no means exhaustive, and they're not meant to be. If your interests end up taking you deeper than this book goes, I encourage you to make use of the vast library the Internet puts at your disposal. You can use the available search engines, such as Google and Yahoo!, to find worlds of information. You're bound to find someone else who has already solved the problem you're having or at least thought about it.

Index

E-F